W9-BFX-203

# LIVING ON LESS

## AND LIKING IT MORE

# LIVING ON LESS AND LIKING IT MORE

## Maxine Hancock

**HARVEST HOUSE PUBLISHERS**
Eugene, Oregon 97402

**Living on Less and Liking It More**

Copyright © 1976 Maxine Hancock
Published 1984 by Harvest House Publishers
Eugene, Oregon 97402

ISBN 0-89081-414-7
Library of Congress Catalog Card Number 76-40220

**All rights reserved.** No portion of this book may be reproduced
in any form without the written permission of the publisher.

**Printed in the United States of America**

To
my parents,
MAX and RUTH RUNIONS,
who have known and shown
that
"godliness with contentment is
great gain"

# CONTENTS

# FIRST, THIS WORD

> In the day of prosperity be joyful, but in the day of adversity consider.
>
> ECCLESIASTES 7:14

This is not a book in praise of poverty, for there is very little about poverty to praise! I like the candor of Samuel Johnson, who said, "While I was running about this town a very poor fellow, I was a great arguer for the advantages of poverty; but I was, at the same time, very sorry to be poor."[1]

All the nostalgic reviving in books and television of the "good old days" when money was scarce but love was plentiful, all the romanticizing of the "pastoral dream" in which folks—more or less effortlessly—just live off the land, leave me very unmoved. For nothing can blot out the fact that poverty is a sharply painful experience. I will have to leave it to others to write chirpily about the joys of voluntary poverty, because we have had a taste of hardship—not that we exactly volunteered for it—and I consider poverty a state to be avoided. I can think of no more appropriate prayer for each other than that recorded by the loving apostle John, "Beloved, I pray that in all respects you may prosper and be in good health, just as your soul prospers" (3 John 2, NASB).

Nevertheless, Cam and I did find "the day of adversity" to be a good time to consider and reconsider—almost ev-

9

erything. Through a jolting business reversal, we came to an understanding of the problems of poverty and the joys of modest living. And we found that modest—and even meager—living could be a way of learning to grow in love.

As young professionals fresh out of the university, we had enjoyed the comfort of regular and adequate wages. And then we decided to farm. Beginning with nothing, we set out bravely in the attempt to borrow the large amount of capital necessary to begin a farming operation. Those first years were rough. But we managed to make payments and meet basic needs, not only for ourselves but for a family to which we were adding every eighteen months or so.

And then, just as we were beginning to get "out of the woods," we saw the opportunity of our lives—that sure thing that was too good to miss. We formed a company with another farming couple and operated a joint grain-and-cattle operation. For three years our grain crops were fed through cattle in the neighbor's feedlot. On paper, it looked great. But just as the big loans we had taken to launch this larger enterprise began to mature and demand repayment, the cattle market slid into a deep depression. We had to sell our fattened beef at prices far below production costs. And suddenly, with the help of an early frost that ruined our crops, we found ourselves eyeball to eyeball with insolvency. What a terrible, frantic, lost, helpless feeling!

Looking back now, we wonder how we would have kept our sanity if we had not been able to laugh—sometimes a kind of near-hysterical bittersweet laughter—at lines like, "Well, one thing is for sure, when a big depression hits, we're going to have had eight years of practice before anyone else gets started." We teased ourselves about the uncertain economics of each of our chosen pursuits. "I guess we're the only two teachers in the country who are trying to subsidize farming with writing," we would say.

A neighbor and his wife, Bill and Mary Karen Bills, convulsed themselves with laughter over Cam's line, delivered one night while he and Bill stood together shivering in the cold fall drizzle while they were drying grain. "Just wish I'd listened to my folks and gone to university," Cam cracked. "Then I could be in somewhere where it's warm."

Through all those hard days, we learned how to live— almost—on love. So for those who are experiencing the acute problems of financial hardship, I hope I can offer some insights and also minister some comfort.

But this book is certainly not in advocacy of poverty. Nor is it against prosperity. The Lord has brought us through our financial crisis—at least that particular one!—and we gladly join the rejoicing psalmist in testifying:

> He brought me up also out of an horrible pit, out of the miry clay, and set my feet upon a rock, and established my goings. (Ps 40:2).

The reflections of this book are written the morning after "the day of adversity." I want to share what we learned through the "considering" forced upon us by adversity, considering which led us to some new thought patterns, some new values, some new attitudes toward our lifestyle. They are attitudes and values we are carrying forward with us, for we now sense God's call to modest living, regardless of our means.

Many of our younger friends are asking tough questions about Christian life-style. Questions like:

"Shouldn't Christian values dematerialize our lives?"

"How do we learn to say, 'Enough's enough?' And at what point should we be saying it?"

"Isn't there more to life than an endless scramble for money and things? Isn't there some way we can learn again how to just live?"

"How will we face Christ as our Judge if we have lived selfishly in a hungry, needy world?"

And this book is for those, too, who are evaluating their life-style in the light of a renewed sense of Christian responsibility.

For those who are hurting financially; for those who are hurting in conscience, uneasily questioning their values and trying to find guidelines for a Christian life-style; and for Cam and for me and for our children, I am writing out of our lives. What this book is about is *modest living*, about learning to live at a somewhat lower standard than that which we had come to accept as the norm in the last thirty years, about finding a balance point between poverty and riches where we can live in love to our Lord, to our families, to our world.

I want to offer some philosophic and scriptural foundations—and some practical guidelines, too—for fellow travelers who, by the front door of idealistic choice or by the back door of "grim necessity," find themselves in modest or even extreme circumstances, and who, by the grace of God, interpret this as a calling, a challenge, a discipline, a ministry.

# 1

# THE CALL TO MODEST LIVING

I first met Abe and Carole Goetz at a mayor's prayer breakfast at which Abe was the featured soloist. When his name was called, I saw him being assisted to the platform, a gaunt, pallid man. At first I thought he must be ill and on the verge of fainting. Then I realized that he was blind. He spoke before he sang, and I have transcribed what he said from a tape of the prayer breakfast program:

> I was asked to say a few words. . . . I would like to say how the Lord really undertakes, even after I lost my sight. It was about a year ago that we moved to Calgary. It was time for school to start, and my wife had earned a little extra money to buy some clothes for the children. She brought it home, and gave it to me to keep so we could go and buy the clothes.
>
> The next morning, the bank phoned. We were $65 overdrawn—just what my wife had brought home. I walked the sixteen blocks to take the money to the bank. Then, with a heavy heart, I came home those sixteen blocks. I knelt and I said, "Lord, You know what we need." And the Lord gave me peace.
>
> Just before my wife came home from work, the mail came. There was a check there for $100. And all it said was, "God bless you." So I want to say, the Lord really does undertake.

As Abe's clear tenor voice carried the melody of "He Touched Me," most of us were digging out handkerchiefs from purses or pockets. We had heard "the sacrifice of praise"—costly praise. It was praise that came out of real hardship. For my part, I wanted to hear more from Abe Goetz and his wife. I wrote to them and received an invitation to visit them in their apartment in Calgary.

The day I went to see them, they were happily enjoying the warmth and comfort of a new living room rug, a Christmas gift from a member of their family. But the clean, neat room was sparsely furnished, and hard times were in evidence. Abe was still getting used to being blind, a result of hemorrhaging caused by diabetes. "It's not black," he explained. "It's just gray." But he couldn't see anything, not even the pretty faces of his little girls rapidly turning into young ladies, nor the face of his wonderful wife, Carole.

I sat there with them, trying to "sit where they sat," trying to imagine how we would react to such a problem. "Didn't you protest? Rebel? Cry out, 'Why me, God?' " I asked.

Abe shook his head. "God is God," he said simply.

And Carole explained, "I think it was harder for me to accept for him than it was for Abe himself. He was really amazing. He just accepted that if this was his lot, he would have to learn to live with it."

They told me, together, of how they had learned lessons in the recent months of financial hardship that they had missed in the earlier years of their married lives.

"Like what?" I asked.

"Like the faithfulness of God. Everything we had ever believed was put to the test, and God is just as good as His Word declares Him to be. Time after time, we would have used our last dollar, and not have any idea where to turn, when the Lord would supply. Once it was by a letter in the mail. Another time—a Sunday morning—a friend pressed a gift of money into our hands when he shook hands with us at the end of the service."

"We learned, too," Abe told me, "how little material things really matter. Before I was blind, things mattered to me. A lot. Like, what kind of car I had, or my clothes." I had looked at the picture on the piano of a big, handsome Abe with his young bride radiant beside him. That other Abe, that Abe "before the darkness," had been a hard-working, self-reliant, things-oriented man. "But now," Abe said, "the only real things are the things of the spirit. I have learned to really *see* in another realm." He was thoughtful for a moment. "And it has made me appreciate my wife more than ever before."

At the time I talked with them, there was still hope that Abe's sight would be restored through another operation—a hope which has since been dashed. But Abe's words still echo in my mind:

"Of course, I hope I'll be able to see again. But I hope that the Lord doesn't give me back my sight until I have learned all that He has to teach me through blindness."

To Abe and Carole—despite all of the financial problems, all the personal readjustments as Carole shouldered wage-earning and Abe took up household tasks—the experience was summed up in this sentence: "To us, this is not a tragedy but an opportunity." They have found in adversity an opportunity to really get to know God, an opportunity to reevaluate things, a new kind of opportunity for service.

Many people, like Abe and Carole, have had to face the economic results of severe illness or disability—a car accident, a kidney failure, a stroke, a heart attack. With the lost earning power come the often overwhelming medical expenses. Such circumstances may force the family to drastically revise its standard of living—sometimes permanently.

Others have had seemingly secure jobs wrenched from them by conditions beyond their control. During the past few years many people who had previously felt secure in their ability to "bring home the bacon" have been forced into the emotional turmoil and economic difficulties accompanying job loss. Not the statistics in *Time* but the happy relief in my friend's voice as she told me, "We're happy—at least Tom still has work and can put the bread on the table—" tells the real tale of the threat of unemployment.

When the breadwinner (or breadwinners) of a family finds himself out of work for even a few weeks or months, the call to modest living cannot be avoided. Many, having lost professional or skilled work, have to accept lower-paying jobs. And the standard of living must, often painfully, be adjusted to the new economic facts of the family's existence.

For others, retirement from the work force brings about an enforced revision—often one that is acutely painful—of their life-style. People who are now entering retirement are those who experienced the struggle of the great depression during the early part of their earning years. Remembering the hard and lean years, they feel sharp anxiety at having once again, in old age and often failing health, to suffer the effects of economic deprivation. This adaptation to a revised standard of living is a difficult adjustment being made by many in the family of God.

Others within the Body of Christ are hearing a less strident but just as unavoidable call to more modest living. For various reasons, many young people are considering seriously a call to a simple life-style. It is a way of freeing themselves from a materialistically motivated "rat race" in which some feel trapped; a way of living for values other than things; a way of conserving the limited resources of our small earth; or a way of making more money from their incomes available for sharing with those in need.

Annabelle and Ron, for instance, have been married for about six years. Both are university graduates. Both have held responsible and remunerative jobs. Now Annabelle has left her university teaching career and is staying at home with their first child, excitedly learning about "child development" (along with "mother development") at close range. Ron is asking himself some hard questions about whether it is worth his while to cling to the high rung of the corporation ladder that he has reached. He has excellent wages as well as opportunities for travel and continuing education with the company for which he works. But his job absorbs his time and energy almost completely. And the company requires that he move periodically from one big city to another, in order to take increasingly responsible jobs.

"There's got to be more to life than this," he says thoughtfully. "I want to supply my family with more than just things. I want to share in their growing up, deeply and intimately." Right now it is just a dream, but Annabelle and Ron are thinking seriously about detaching themselves from his job, with all its opportunity and bounty, and living modestly on a lower wage so that together they can enjoy more of the tasks of being parents.

Other young people have set the example. Will Pattison left a responsible civil service post a few years back. Now he and his wife, Marion, each work very limited part-time hours—she at teaching nursing; he, as an economic consultant—to create a modest, pooled "living allowance." The rest of their energy is going into creating a simple life-style on a small farm. Both having grown up in the country, they know what they are doing and what sacrifices are required. "We can live together as a family this way," they say. "The children can know the joy of finding new kittens in the loft, and we can share that joy with them."

Thus, a new appreciation of the real needs of families is creating a call to more modest living for some. Another growing realization that is forcing itself upon our thinking is that the luxurious life-style which has been so generally adopted is, in large measure, responsible for the ecological problems we now face. Francis Schaeffer sees "hurry and greed" as the dual cause of most ecological damage:

> *Almost always,* the scar and the ugliness are the results of hurry. And whether it is hurry or greed, these things eat away at nature. But as Christians we have to learn to say "Stop!" Because . . . greed is destructive against nature at this point and there is a time to take one's time.[1]

With this awareness, many young people are altering their life-styles, attempting to reduce their own personal consumption of the earth's depleted resources. I recently heard a radio program on the "Ecologically Ideal Family," a family that uses few cans, separates recyclable wastepaper from that destined for burning, uses washable wipe-up rags and handkerchiefs, and bikes or walks whenever possible. Such a family may well be the prototype of the new-style Christian family who recognizes its responsibility for the wise and conservative use of this planet's limited resources.

Then, too, some young people are taking steps to live on less than what they earn in order that they might have more to share. In a Midwestern city, a doctor and his wife recently sold their large home in an exclusive district and relocated in a modest house in a working-man's section of the same city. They chose to drive a plain and aging car. They began to grow a garden. Now, with an income much larger than their reduced family needs, they are able to give generously to missions, world relief, and their local church. To them, the call of Jesus Christ was to a more modest life-style. They heard and responded with obedience.

While not all believers are being called to take such drastic action to change their life-styles, many are looking for ways to trim the budget, to be more conservative in their spending, and thus, either to reduce their personal needs in order to live comfortably on a lower income, leaving them more time and energy for other pursuits compatible with their Christian commitment, or to leave themselves a wider margin of income over needs, from which they can share more bountifully with others.

The fact is that the Christian Church in North America, which had become bogged down in the things-based value system which until recently dominated Western culture, is awakening to other values. The impact of the Jesus People, for instance, is being felt. Most of us could ignore the antimaterialistic social comment made by the hippy movement until we were faced with the dedication and simplicity of life of the committed, "dematerialized" Jesus People who became the conscience of the movement and, in a sense, of the Church. Now, more and more, Christians are becoming uncomfortably aware that some of the very basic principles of Christianity were sold or traded cheaply at a garage sale of values in this century and the last. We are struggling back toward an emphasis on such things as love and compassion and costly sharing.

While we may reject as economically simplistic some of the alternative life-styles being tried, and while we may reject as sociologically unrealistic some of the alternative structures (such as communal living) which are being experimented with, still, none of us is immune from the underlying values that are being rediscovered, or at least

reemphasized. We are being reminded that we have no
right to settle down into comfortable complacency. We are
remembering our identity as "strangers and pilgrims" (1
Pe 2:11).

Unfortunately, perhaps, we cannot hail this new sen-
sitivity to other than material values with the optimism of
Charles A. Reich, who sees in the antimaterialistic life
view of the flower children a whole new "consciousness"
which will result in a new cultural flowering, new life-
styles, and ultimately, "the greening of America."[2]

As we read the Word of God, we are too aware of the Fall
of man to fall for such an attractive but unfounded concept.
We are aware of the need of each human heart for something far more radical than a change of "consciousness": of
our need for personal redemption and renewal through the
grace of God, extended to us as we place our faith in the
Lord Jesus Christ. Nonetheless, as Christians we should be
gratefully aware of a change in mood concerning things, a
change which is forcing many of us to do some serious
reevaluating.

In various ways and for various reasons, many of us are
reawakening to the warning of our Lord: "Beware of
covetousness: for a man's life consisteth not in the abun-
dance of the things which he possesseth" (Lk 12:15).
That's a verse I memorized in the tongue-twisting King
James Version as a junior in Sunday school. I worked then
to wrap my tongue around the difficult sounds. I am still
working at wrapping my mind around the far more complex concepts it states so tersely.

The call to modest living is a call that is being heard by
many today. How to respond to that call, how to readjust
values and reeducate tastes, and how to learn new habits
and acquire new attitudes: that is the subject of the chap-
ters that follow.

# 2

# THE GOLDEN MEAN

I could hardly believe my eyes. But there, entering the sun-filled doorway of our little church with her uncle and aunt, was Marilyn McKerihan. I thought she was in Haiti, but she was *really* there in flesh and blood in our Alberta village, looking more beautiful than ever after a year of working with Radio Lumière in Haiti. As I greeted her, I learned that she had come home for a reunion with members of her family who serve the Lord in many parts of the world.

"Well, come on down to my class," I invited after I had pinched myself a couple of times to really believe she was there. "I've got the high school girls. Come and tell us about what you have been doing."

Marilyn's visit with our high school class was memorable. "You can't imagine how the average person lives in Haiti," she said. "You just can't. The average person expects to get about three meals a week."

"A week?" we echoed uncomprehendingly, hoping she had made a mistake.

"A week!" she reiterated.

She was quite right; there was no way we could imagine such hunger. The girls and I asked Marilyn numerous questions, probing many aspects of her missionary experi-

ence. We knew her to be a gifted and well-trained pianist.
"Are you teaching piano lessions?" we asked.

"Oh no," she said. "There's no point. It's so far beyond
the most unrealistic dream of a Haitian ever to be able to
afford a piano that there is no point in teaching them how
to play it. The things we could use are some secondhand
guitars in reasonable condition. With those, they could
bring some music into their homes."

She described the poverty, the 90 percent illiteracy rate,
the health problems. "It's just hopeless, hopeless, hopeless!" she exclaimed. Yet, she was going back.

Since that Sunday morning, I have rarely sat down to my
old, moving-scarred piano without remembering what
Marilyn said. And often when we sit down as a family for
our third meal of the day, we remember that there are those
who are glad if they have three meals a week, and realize
that even in the most extreme circumstances we have
faced, we have been—by the standards of the greatest part
of the world—lavishly wealthy.

And so, in discussing "modest living," we run into an
immediate difficulty. Just what is it? "Modest" compared
with what? Where do we draw the line? At what point do
we say "satisfied"? And by whose standard of comparison
are we entitled to call our life-style modest? Do we measure our life-style against that of the Haitians? Or the
hungry of North Africa or Bangladesh? Yet, how can we
ignore the economic realities of the Western world which
have given us such a high standard of living? Do we have
to live in either self-inflicted poverty or self-induced guilt?

Stanley Tam, an enormously successful businessman
who has lived modestly and devoted his business profits to
the Lord's work, makes this telling comment:

> I am not a sackcloth-and-ashes Christian. We have a modest
> but comfortable home. My wife and I dress well. We are

careful with money, never lavish in our spending. . . . It is
characteristic of Americans—too often including American Christians—to adjust their living standards to their
amount of income, usually keeping the former just a bit
higher than the latter. But really, in this land which offers
so much, where the poorest family in almost any community has more than the wealthiest family in some overseas
areas . . . the thinking Christian needs to consider carefully
that point at which he will be willing to say, "It is good
enough."[1]

How do we, individually and as families, avoid becoming sackcloth-and-ashes Christians and yet enter into the
joys of modest living? The voice of wisdom speaks to us
from the book of Proverbs: "Give me neither poverty nor
riches; feed me with the food that is my portion" (Pr 30:8,
NASB). The dangers of either extreme are summarized in
this same passage:

> Lest I be full and deny Thee and say, "Who is the LORD?" Or
> lest I be in want and steal, And profane the name of my God
> (v. 9).

In wealth, the danger is independence of God. In poverty,
the danger is the temptation to "curse God, and die" (Job
2:9).

What we are looking for in this whole consideration of
modest living is something like the ancient Greek
philosophical idea of the golden mean, that perfect balance point at which there is neither too much nor too little
of anything. The New Testament refined this concept,
telling us that, as believers, a hallmark should be "modera-
tion" (Phil 4:5) or "temperance" (Gal 5:23). As believers,
we have not only the challenge, but the indwelling power
of the Holy Spirit, to enable us to live at that golden mean
so long sought by pagan philosophers, that golden mean at
which we have neither too much nor too little, but at which

we have brought needs and supply into a comfortable balance. In our affluent society, that golden mean or balance point will probably best be reached through generous sharing of the good things with which we have been blessed.

Before we begin feeling a bit smug about the level at which we establish our own personal golden mean, we need to remind ourselves of the golden standard by which all giving, all cutting back, all sharing, must ultimately be measured:

> For you know the grace of our Lord Jesus Christ, that though He was rich, yet for your sake He became poor, that you through His poverty might become rich (2 Co 8:9, NASB).

I would like to suggest three basic principles on which a life-style of modest living can be based:

1. *Responsibility:* The concept of stewardship of all of our personal resources is central to any meaningful Christian commitment. And, of course, the idea that all that we have in material goods or in talents and abilities is a gift to be held in trust, carries with it the concept of accountability for how we use those gifts. "It is required of stewards," Paul writes, "that one be found trustworthy" (1 Co 4:2, NASB).

Any idea that money—or what we do with it—is not a spiritual matter, that it does not concern God, lacks scriptural foundation. Harold J. Sutton has pointed out that "money and possessions are allotted much space in the Bible. In the Old Testament, it is one verse in six; in the New Testament it is one verse in seven. Sixteen of the parables of our Lord have to do with the stewardship of possessions."[2]

The parable of the talents (Mt 25:14-30) is Jesus' classic

discourse on the requirements and responsibilities of
stewardship. What we are given we must use—not for our
own satisfaction—but for maximum profit to the Giver.
Those of us who are blessed in living in the wealthy West
will have to answer for our use of that wealth. Have we
squandered it? Dug a hole and hid it by failing to invest it
in the lives of others? Or are we recognizing the trust
which is ours, and the fact that we will answer for our use
of material wealth, by using our money wisely and invest-
ing it for spiritual returns?

The parable of the talents can also be seen to refute the
idea of a leveling approach to money matters. The Master,
as He saw fit, gave varying amounts—all in trust—to His
servants. The early Christian community in which the
saints "had all things in common" (see Ac 2:44, NASB)
seems to have been a rather short-lived social experiment.
Communal or "leveled income" living is not recommended to other church groups in the letters of Paul.
Indeed, in those letters, individual responsibility is
stressed, each man being told to work to support his own
family and share with those in need. It is evident from the
epistles that there were rich and poor people together in
the churches. To some, in the early days of the Church, the
call of the Master was to "sell all that you possess, and
distribute it to the poor . . . and come, follow Me" (Lk 18:22,
NASB). To others, the call was to faithfully administer the
wealth they had to the glory of God. And so it will be today.

But regardless of how much or little we are entrusted
with, we will all give answer for our use of income, not
only annually, when we answer to the Internal Revenue
Service, but ultimately when we stand at the judgment seat
of Christ. The commendation, "Well done, thou good and
faithful servant," (Mt 25:21) is for those who have understood the twin concepts of stewardship and accountability, and have fulfilled the responsibility of wise manage-

ment of the material things with which they have been entrusted.

2. *Restraint:* Living modestly by choice means living somewhere below the level that could be maintained if all of your income were administered for the family's needs and wants.

Years ago, when deep freezes came onto the general public market, I remember a discussion in our home about purchasing one. With a growing family to feed, my frugal mother could see the obvious economic advantages of owning a home deep freeze. Mother and Dad discussed the deep freeze two or three times. Each time, the discussion died away and did not resurface for several months. Finally, a family-sized deep freeze was bought. I just assumed that my parents had purchased the freezer as soon as they could afford it. Because they were people who did not let their right hand know what their left hand was doing, I didn't stumble onto the truth until much later in a conversation with my mother. "Of course," she commented, "we could have had a deep freeze long before we bought one."

"Why didn't you get it earlier?" I pressed.

My mother shrugged. "Because several times when we had the money laid aside for the freezer, the Lord brought to our attention someone who had a greater need."

That's restraint. And it results in modest living.

Modest living is refusing to be coerced, by television and other advertising, into feeling that everything five years or older is obsolete and in need of replacement. But it does not necessarily mean living in a deprived state. It simply means recognizing that income entrusted to a family is its to administer for the glory of God. And that will require restraint in personal spending.

3. *Realism:* Modest living requires a strong sense of

realism, something often dulled by easy credit and high-pressure advertising. It means living within our limited budgets, whether they are limited of necessity or by choice. In a local department store, many items bear the tag: "Want it? Charge it!" With such encouragement, it is possible for a family to live perpetually beyond its means, keeping up an appearance of prosperity in excess of real earnings. When hard times come or tighter budgeting is chosen, it is important to forget about trying to kid anyone—especially yourselves—about the economic realities of your new life-style.

Modest living means that, even within our most limited means, we recognize our obligation to our hungry and needy world neighbors, and to those of our world who still have not heard the Gospel. There is no financial state in which the responsibility of giving is lifted from us. The writers of the gospels record the unforgettable comment of our Lord as He stood watching people bring their money gifts to the Temple. After a number of wealthy people had made large, clinking donations, a poverty-stricken widow put in "two mites" and Jesus said, "This poor widow put in more than all the contributors to the treasury; for they all put in out of their surplus, but she, out of her poverty, put in all she owned, all she had to live on" (Mk 12:43-44, NASB). Giving from our wealth and plenty is one kind of giving, but giving from our poverty—giving from our very day-to-day necessities, sharing our "daily bread"—this kind of giving is especially commended by our Lord. Realism demands that we stop using the term "sacrificial giving" glibly, and that we learn the deep pain and real joy of giving that affects our living.

Modest living also means to "walk honestly toward them that are without" (1 Th 4:12). It means living with a sense of realism and responsibility toward our creditors, both in undertaking and discharging debt obligations.

Realism in modest living means recognizing the material needs of those who depend upon us. "If any one does not provide for his own, and especially for those of his household, he has denied the faith, and is worse than an unbeliever" (1 Ti 5:8, NASB) is Paul's strong statement on the matter. We must assess and realistically provide for the needs of our children and, in some cases, those of our aging parents. Such provision has an indisputable a priori claim on our "charity." Some of Jesus' harshest words were to those who failed to help needy parents and excused themselves by saying, "Corban," that is, by claiming that their money was dedicated to some religious purpose (see Mk 7:11-12). As we more and more frequently encounter the neglect of old people by their families, we as Christians need to stress the importance of honoring the needs of our own kin.

Basically, then, modest living is an orientation toward income and life-style rather than a specific point on the line between poverty and wealth. No single inflexible standard can be set, for what is modest living for people with a large earning power may still be out of reach for others with less. The concept of modest living should not suggest that there is anything wrong with enjoying the good things of life as they are entrusted to us. I have praised God, sometimes even composing psalms of thanks to Him, for my automatic appliances, because of the hours they have freed me from household work for other pursuits.

Living in a very cramped, although picturesque, rented house, Cam and I look forward to God's provision of a big enough home for our family of four fast-growing children. When He does supply the house, we will move into it with thanksgiving and joy. Nagging feelings of guilt about physical comforts should be banished if, first of all, the good things we have are not received at the expense of others; and second, if the good things we enjoy are truly within our means and are not just a result of setting ourselves adrift on a sea of credit.

Modest living is not so much a renunciation of specific things in themselves as it is a renunciation of making "things" a goal in life or a source of satisfaction to us. It is the exercise of responsibility, of restraint, and of realism, whether our means are large or small.

While he was moderator of the United Church of Canada, Dr. Robert McClure compared the unhappiness he found etched on the faces of the drivers of cars on a traffic-jammed Canadian street with the mass misery of the hungry crowds on the streets of cities in India where he had served as a medical missionary. He concluded that too much money made people just as miserable as too little money; that there was probably a happy medium at which basic needs could be met without a pinch, but at which the endless grabbing for things was out of reach. And that happy medium, he felt, would be most conducive to human happiness.

We need to fight our way back to such a happy medium as a balance point for our economic lives. We need to find the golden mean. And we will start heading back toward it as we really face the fact that the only real satisfactions in life do not come from reaching for or in getting things but in living in fellowship with our Creator, and in sharing His life and love with others around us. We can only enter into this fellowship through faith in the Lord Jesus Christ. And the satisfaction it brings is internal, unaffected by external circumstances. It was such internal satisfaction that Jesus offered to the woman at the well outside of Sychar, when He said,

> Everyone who drinks of this water shall thirst again; but whoever drinks of the water that I shall give him shall

never thirst; but the water that I shall give him shall become in him a well of water springing up to eternal life (Jn 4:13-14, NASB).

Long centuries before Jesus sat on the edge of the well and conversed with the heart-hungry woman, the prophet Jeremiah had used the "well image" to describe the unsatisfied state of God's people in his day. "My people have committed two evils," Jeremiah said, speaking on behalf of the Lord God. "They have forsaken me the fountain of living waters, and hewed them out cisterns, broken cisterns, that can hold no water" (Jer 2:13).

Cam grew up in a farm home which had no reliable source of water. There were ground wells, the kind that were shallow and constantly going dry. And there was a cistern in the basement. It didn't leak as did the ones Jeremiah described, but it did run out of water from time to time. Dishes were habitually done in a few inches of water in the bottom of a dishpan. Bath water had to be shared by two or three family members.

But then there came a day when Cam's folks invested in the drilling of a deep well, one that went down past the surface water streams and into the deep-flowing subterranean river, and hence it could simply not be pumped dry. What a change in that old farmhouse! Indoor plumbing, running water, the luxury of a shower, and a bathtub in which one could lounge.

Could you imagine them, linked to such a supply of water, abandoning the use of that deep well and returning to the sponge-bath, water-scrimping days? Can you imagine them turning off the deep-well pump and drawing water out of the old cistern?

Yet many of God's people here in our affluent society have done just that. Declaring, singing, and constantly being reminded that "Jesus Is the Answer," they nonetheless rely heavily on "things" to bring them satisfaction. And when interest in one "toy" or "trinket" wanes, they quickly reach for the next. And the next. And the next. In the preoccupations of life, many of God's people are not distinguishable from those who do not profess to know Him.

Because of the sophistication and ubiquity of advertising which encourages us to indulge, to satisfy our limitless taste for luxury, to "covet greedily all the day long" (Pr 21:26), every one of us in this society is in danger of losing his true perspective. We are in constant danger of being "conformed to this world." It is only as we come daily to the Word of God that we can be "transformed by the renewing of . . . [our] mind" (Ro 12:2) so that, resting in God's loving fatherhood, we can accept the good things He grants us with thanksgiving and gratitude, while sharing openhandedly and with a deep sense of responsibility. We will experience the deep flow of satisfaction only when we link ourselves by faith to the very life of Christ, living out a recognition of this basic principle of stewardship: "Freely ye have received, freely give" (Mt 10:8).

# 3

# CONTENTMENT: LEARNED, NOT EARNED

"Maxine?" The voice on the other end of the phone was one I loved to hear.

"Margie!" I responded. "Oh, I'm so glad you called!" I was answering the phone from my bed, although it was the middle of the day. I had been sick for several weeks and was getting no better, en route to major surgery but not knowing it at the time. I had written a little note to my sister-in-law, Marg Jones. It must have sounded desperate, because she replied with a "prime time" long-distance phone call. Talking with her was a lift I needed just then.

We chatted about several things, including my health, or lack of it, and the things she was concerned about. "You know," she told me, "I get so cross at myself. I seem to have such an awful battle with keeping content. But I noticed something the other day that helped. You know, Paul says, 'I have learned how to get along happily whether I have much or little. . . . I have learned the secret of contentment in every situation.' " Marg read the verse from *The Living Bible*, Philippians 4:11-12. She went on: "When I read that the other day, the word that stuck out at me was 'learned.' Maybe it didn't come any easier to Paul to be content than it does to any of us, but it is a lesson that *can* be learned."

Marg was right, of course. Contentment does not come easily to our hearts, for since Adam's Fall, in the emptiness of the human spirit we have been things-oriented. But contentment can be learned. And in learning it, we have the master Teacher, God's Holy Spirit, to instruct us.

Contentment is probably the closest state in the world to happiness, that greatly sought-after but always elusive goal. It is a quiet plateau that can be reached internally even when there seems little external reason for it. But it is a difficult lesson to learn, because our own natures and our enemy, Satan, keep us in a constant state of "just one thing more." We're not quite content, but we know that if only we had just one more thing, we would be.

Of course, like all of Satan's other lies, this is a delusion, designed to keep us perpetually unhappy, perpetually off-balance, perpetually more concerned about things than we are concerned about God. If you asked a group of young couples what stood in the way of complete contentment, you would probably find it expressed in terms of just simple, single things:

"If only we had a bigger house (or apartment)."

"If only we earned another $200 a month, we could make it."

"If only I could afford a new coat."

"If only we could get a new rug for the living room." And all of these sighs of "if only" fail to take into account that as we move into that bigger house, as we earn that larger income, as we wear that new coat, and as we walk on that new rug, we are still basically the same people. And the inward sigh of bitterness and discontent, "If only we had—" will still be on our lips, but with another ending. The whole thing moves like a game of musical chairs. We move into the next position, only to get ready to jump and move again, and again, and again. Any concept of contentment which is linked to specific things is fallacious. The person who thinks that some specific thing finally will bring him to that plateau called contentment is being deluded, I believe, by Satan, that master deceiver who since the Garden of Eden has been whispering his urgings to the human heart to reach, reach, reach, and take.

As I am writing these lines, my four-year-old is speaking to me from the kitchen where he is folding up newspapers he had spread out on the floor for spatter painting. "What is it, Mitchell?" I call.

He walks into the room where I am typing, holding a folded newspaper and studying an ad wistfully. "I wish we had a snowmobile," he says. And I sigh deep down inside, realizing how hard it is for those of our rich generation to enter the kingdom of spiritual values and to really understand how little *things* do mean.

My memory flashes back to the days, soon after we had completed our studies at the university, when Cam thought aloud, "I wish I had a snowmobile." They were fairly new on the popular market then, and in our long, snowy winters it's not hard to rationalize a "need" for such a recreational vehicle. Cam was earning a good wage; he was entitled to what our nephew Terry Evans once called "a man's toy." But it wasn't long before the possibilities of the "toy" were exhausted. And every snowdrift started to look like every other snowdrift, and every race to feel like every other race. The snowmobile—finally sold to someone else—stands in our minds as a lifelong reminder of how unsatisfying individual things are.

One of the most content men I know is Al Jones. (He's my young sister-in-law's husband, and maybe part of her trouble with learning to be content is just that he is *so* content!) We knew Al long before Margie did, as a member of a youth group that Cam and I sponsored in Edmonton. Then, just as he was maturing into manhood, Al was involved in a near-fatal traffic accident. For a time it was dubious that he would live. And for a while after that, there was doubt that he would ever walk again. But Al *did* walk again! I remember seeing his tall, handsome frame, thin and bent over as he struggled to church again, first walking with two canes. And then the canes were put aside and Al gradually convalesced into vigorous manhood, carrying his six foot four frame like a football pro. But there's something different about Al from other young men of his age. Al is living—virtually—on the other side of death. He knows that he almost died. And he recognizes the value of living above the value of things.

It is interesting that a similar experience brought author David Grayson to write his little book, *Adventures in Contentment*. It's an old book, published in 1906, and a quaint one. But it contains this concept of "living on the other side of death" as a key to contentment. Grayson tells how, from the age of seventeen, he was driven "always forward, toward that vague Success which we Americans love to glorify."[1] Then a very serious illness arrested him, and he dropped out of the rat race into a much slower existence. He says,

> I remember walking in the sunshine, weak yet, but curiously satisfied. I that was dead lived again. . . . And I possessed . . . a knowledge of a former existence, which I knew, even then, I could never return to.

His basic discoveries on which he built this contentment were:

> That we are not, after all, the slaves of things . . . that we are not the used, but the users; that life is more than profit or loss.[2]

Contentment is really—as experienced by these two young men after close scrapes with death, and as experienced by Christians down through the ages—a matter of

living on the other side of death. It is only as we come to
understand Paul's words, "I have been crucified with
Christ; and it is no longer I who live, but Christ lives in me"
(Gal 2:20, NASB) that we come to understand how foolish
our attachment to and our craving for "things" really becomes.

Some of us—like me—are slow learners. We seem to
have to "die" a little every day. Perhaps there are ways of
shortening the learning process, of leaping to the mature
understanding of how trivial things of this world are and
how meaningless are the little toys for which we strive and
struggle. For Al Jones, the shortcut was a face-off with
death itself. For some it may be a dark night of the soul in
which we learn full surrender and cry out, "All that I have
and am and want, I give to You, my Lord and Master."
Perhaps for the rest of us it has to be a matter of taking the
things one at a time, as they present themselves to our
minds in a delusion of delight, and dying to them—
literally dying to the desire for that particular thing. And
then, as one thing after another is passed by and we die to
the desire that was kindled within us, we will gradually
reach a habit of laying things before God without the long
struggle of soul.

Cam and I call this attitude "Holding things on an open
hand." We remember how one of our children had, as a
toddler, clutched a piece of candy we had asked her not to
take. Such defiant, tightly curled little round fingers! We
think of how we had to pry those little fingers, one by one,
away from that treasure and take the candy from her in
order to teach obedience. It would have been so much
easier for her—and for us—if she had held that goody out
to us on an open hand and let us take it.

Job showed the attitude of "holding things on an open
hand" when he cried out, "The LORD gave, and the LORD
hath taken away; blessed be the name of the LORD" (Job

1:21). The earlier in life we learn to stop grabbing, clutching, and holding tightly, and the sooner we learn to hold
all of life's good things in an open hand, the more easily
and gently God can deal with us as His children. That's
another way of saying that the more we live "on the other
side of death," as Paul describes it in Romans 6, the less we
will be attached to temporal, material things.

I will always remember the Sunday when Garth Ford,
the usher on our aisle in church, held the offering basket
out to our family. He noticed that little Heather Ruth,
barely two at the time, was clutching something tightly.
Assuming that she had been given money to be put in the
plate, he held it quietly in front of her. Blue-eyed, round-
cheeked Heather looked gravely from the plate to the
usher, then down to her tightly clenched fist. And then,
just as gravely, she moved her hand over the offering plate
and let go what she was holding. Garth was as startled as I
was to see, lying in the offering basket, a tiny paper figure
of a blue-swaddled baby Moses—a treasured item from the
take-home things she had been given in Sunday school.
We smiled—but with tears just back of our eyes—for
Heather Ruth had opened her hand to give something very
precious to her.

I have found in many instances that God has waited
patiently for us to move some desire from a position of
central importance to the fringes of our minds—in short,
no matter how reasonable or precious, to let it go—before
He was able to let us have that very item. He seems to grant
"things" only when we are living relative to them, "on the
other side of death," dead to them as goals, as status sym-
bols, as sources of satisfaction, and accepting them only as
means of bringing pleasure and praise to the One who has
created all things (see Rev 4:11).

Maybe one of the deepest instincts in a woman is a
nesting instinct: a desire to have a suitable place in which

to raise her brood. As a European friend put it: "For myself, I care not at all about things. Pff! You can have anything I have; I do not care. But for my children, it is different. Children turn one into a bourgeois." This instinct is right and proper. Yet, like all of our good basic instincts, it can be turned against us and against God if we do not guard our lives carefully. Our need for a nesting place can become an obsession. Our definition of "adequate" can be raised to levels to which we may have no right by merely turning the pages of *Better Homes and Gardens* or by driving through those mouth-watering "exclusive" areas of our cities.

When we moved out to the old farmhouse where Cam had been raised, I said to him, "Don't ever ask me to move again." I put my roots down, right alongside the towering pine that stood close to the front veranda. The house was old, at least in western Canadian terms. It had been built soon after the turn of the century, and a lean-to had been added somewhere along the way. The kitchen occupied the lean-to, with a floor so sloped that anything which spilled landed up against the south baseboards. Upstairs were two bedrooms, both built under the eaves with steeply sloping walls; a tiny niche which in the old days had been—in the most strictly limited sense of the word—a *bath*room; and a walk-in closet or "drying room" with a tiny windowed dormer. Into this upstairs we tucked ourselves with first three and then four children, turning the niche into crib space and later building a double-decker bunk into it and painting and papering the closet to make a tiny bedroom off ours for Cammie-Lou.

There were saving virtues about the old place with its torn screens and loose windowpanes. Such as a large living room which, despite a sagging ceiling that made us wonder just what day the upstairs would come downstairs, had a fieldstone fireplace; a lovely big bathroom-utility room on the main floor, created out of one of the downstairs bedrooms when the house had been "modernized" late in its career. And, best of all, a downstairs bedroom adjoining the living room, that worked perfectly for a study-office for me. Outside, the old house was peeling, the veranda sagging. But inside, there was warmth and love and happiness. And while I racked my brains trying to think of ways to expand our living space around the needs of our growing children, I had no intention of moving. Ever.

And then Cam, who had been increasingly distressed with a continuous hay fever reaction, went to an allergist. Skin tests were done, and the allergist was ready with his diagnosis. "Do you by any chance live in an old house?" he asked. Cam nodded. Yes, we lived in an old house.

"Ah!" the allergist exclaimed. "There's your problem. You are allergic to the sort of molds which accumulate in the walls of old houses, especially walls where moisture can seep in. Your strongest reaction is to such molds. I strongly advise that you get into a new house."

The doctor's diagnosis and prescription shattered my contentment. If Cam was sick in the house we lived in, and if a new house was necessary to his good health, wasn't it obvious that the Lord had indicated that we should build a new house? Obvious—to me. Not so obvious, unfortunately, to Cam.

Because what was more obvious to Cam than it was to me was that the business was going badly. That we were selling cattle at a loss. That we had debts that were going to be hard to meet. And Cam, man of integrity that he is, could not face building a new house—even on doctor's orders—while telling people that he could not afford to pay his bills. And so we were stalemated. For the first time in our marriage, our ability to communicate and to come to an understanding seemed to break down completely.

And then, the Lord provided us with a house.

Not, like in some people's stories, a big, new house that somehow a kindly rich person had a sudden need to sell at some inexplicably low price. Nothing like that. God provided an *old* house, squarer and better built than our previous one, even more picturesque, and for rent. I, who had framed my request to the Lord as my "Three S Prayer"—for space, settledness, and security—found myself moving from one old farmhouse to another old farmhouse about a third smaller; from one where I felt sure I could live out my life to one in which we would have three months' notice if a member of the landlord's family needed it; from one which we owned, to one which we could only rent. Talk about insecurity! I felt like a hen that couldn't quite settle back on the nest for fear it might suddenly be jerked away from under her.

If the tears had flowed as I walked down the winter lane of our own home, trying to figure out how to cope with Cam's illness and adamantine attitude about building a new home, now I found them starting without notice as I tried to get things tucked into this latest domicile. I somehow could not reconcile myself to this as the Lord's way of answering my prayer.

To make things worse, the house we moved into had a "reputation." It had belonged to a well-to-do city businessman who lived in the country. And since it was set well back from the road, down a pine-lined drive and in a beautiful parklike yard, people thought I was wonderfully lucky to be moving into such a grand house. "That's a beautiful big old house," they would comment.

"Beautiful, yes," I would reply. But big, definitely not. My hardest adjustment was having no study to work in. My filing cabinets were out in the unheated veranda; my desk and typewriter were stuffed into our small bedroom alongside the bed. That was harder for me to cope with than the ten by thirteen foot combination kitchen-dining room with *five* doors leading off it!

Why? Why? Why? What could possibly make this move right? Trying to make the best of things, I buoyed myself up through each week. We had moved closer to the center of the farming operation, so Cam could be home for lunch and supper with us. That was fun, especially since for the previous two years he had left early in the morning and not returned until ten o'clock or later at night all through the cropping season, becoming a virtual stranger to the children. And his allergy symptoms were definitely less acute. I was grateful for those things. Yet, each Sunday, when the kids had excused themselves after dinner and were out playing in the yard and Cam and I still sat across the table that took up about half of the tiny—although very pretty and freshly painted—kitchen, the tears would come. And the questions. And the anger. And the retorts. Cam was immovable. He could not see that we could afford to build a house.

And then one Sunday afternoon, I walked away from the table in anger. There wasn't very far that I could go in the house to get away from Cam, but I went into the bedroom adjoining the kitchen and threw myself, sobbing, onto the bed. And then, as I quieted down, things began to come into focus for me.

First of all, such unhappiness was definitely not coming from the Lord.

Second, I had written a book entitled *Love, Honor, and Be Free*, not yet published at that time, but accepted for publication, in which I had urged the wife to submit to her husband. And here I was, angry and unsubmissive and wretchedly unhappy.

And then, the gift of imagination helped me see into a possible future. I imagined what it would be like if I did coerce Cam into complying with my wish for a new home.

Suppose we went ahead and built? Suppose then, that as Cam now feared, the house became a fearful financial burden? And suddenly I could picture us growing apart in a house big enough for us to really get apart from each other, and with Cam's love for me killed by my demands. And just imagining any size or shape of house without the love and joy, which had been our mainstay through all the "better and worse" situations since we had been married, was convincing to me.

I talked with my Lord first. And it wasn't easy. But I said, "Lord, I don't feel submissive. I feel that my reasoning is sound and right. But I will to submit to Cam. And I am willing to allow that You can communicate to him our need for a new home without my badgering." I lay there for a while until my heart felt still and calm, and then I walked out to the kitchen.

Cam was still nursing his cup of tepid tea with a hurt, bewildered, and angry look on his face. I sat down and took his hand, the big, square, capable hand I had loved at first sight so many years before. "Cam," I said, "I'm all finished. I've said everything I'm going to say about 'house.' You won't hear me say a word about it until you say it first."

From the moment that I submitted and gave up—first to God and then to my husband in this area of my quite legitimate desire—joy began to flow back into my life. The little house was no less crowded, but now I could enjoy its charm and beauty. No longer threatened by my demands, Cam was able to begin to share his problems and concerns with me, and communication between us became the deep, intimate sharing we had known before. I learned, again, that love and contentment are all that are really necessary to turn an "inadequate" house into a happy home.

The next few months fully vindicated Cam's determination not to assume any further debt for a house. When the farming business failed—an outcome that I had not realized was as imminent as Cam had—we were set to weather a financial storm that could have completely capsized us had we also been trying to pay for a new home. Our personal credibility with our creditors was high because we were living stringently, and they were remarkably patient with us. The little rented house was inexpensive to heat, which helped to keep our living costs to a minimum. And all through that winter, the long hard winter of psychological restoration after a business failure, we thanked God for our snug and inexpensive accommodation. Debt we faced. Problems we had. But, as we lived close together in the small house, we experienced the joy of simple things: of enough money to buy a week's groceries, of enough money to pay the month's rent, of peace and joy and love between ourselves. What might have been "the winter of our discontent"—apart from the transforming work of the Holy Spirit—we shall always remember as the "winter of our deep content."

In our financial setback, the Lord weeded out from Cam's heart, one by one, things that had become too dear to him. The big tractors and trucks and equipment had to be sold as we liquidated assets to try to cover liabilities. And, at the same time, just as relentlessly, the great Gardener weeded from my heart the need, the burning desire, for a big new house. I can now say with Paul, "I have learned how to get along happily whether I have much or little." On some matters, at least, we are living "on the other side of death."

I am not pretending that the learning process has been fun or easy. But the Spirit of God is a thorough and loving Teacher. And of all the joys of life, it is contentment—that quiet, happy plateau of the spirit—for which I am most grateful. It is contentment which I most jealously guard from the attacks that come on it in a thousand reasonable and attractive guises.

I know many people at many levels of income who are inwardly gnawed by discontent. And I know many others, also at many levels of income, who enjoy quiet contentment. I am convinced that contentment cannot be earned. But I know, from experience, that it can be learned.

# 4

# LIVING ON LOVE

You can't live on love.

But it's even harder to live without it.

And when a family—by choice or of necessity—cuts back its standard of living, it dare not lower its standard of loving. Love is not that "now you have it, now you don't" emotion which is crooned or yelled about in today's songs. Love is the glue that sticks people together. And often, economic hardship is an experience that proves, and improves, love more than any other experience could. Of course, it can work the other way, too. Economic problems are cited as a major contributing factor in a high percentage of marriage breakdowns. So, if you are facing financial rough weather for whatever reason, you need to make sure your marriage is ready for the gales.

One of the first things essential to "living on love" is clear and honest communication. This communication must first exist between the partners in the marriage itself. If a couple feels God's call to exercise restraint in their life-style in order to give more or live more or love more, they need to work out carefully together to what level they plan to reduce their spending. Realism is very important here. No matter how altruistic you are, you still have to exist within some segment of the North American culture.

Crushing financial worries are no boon. You should not make your restraint become an experience of "hair-shirting," but rather, base your cutbacks on a realistic estimate of your needs as a family unit.

If a husband and wife do not share fully the goals for which they are reducing their standard of living, it is hard to avoid bitterness between them. When Bob, a prosperous city dentist, decided to give up his practice to assume a church-related ministry, his wife found the "call" hard to accept. "It's a full-time job he's taking on," Aileen told me, "at a half-time salary." Because she was a submissive wife, Aileen went along with the change in life-style, but she found the personal adjustments very difficult. Obviously, it is incumbent upon men who feel God's call to a ministry which entails a reduced income to fully and deeply share their reasons and purposes with their wives who must share the "simple life" with them.

If the cutback is not one of choice, but one which is forced upon you, then clear and complete honesty in communications becomes even more imperative. The hardest honesty of all is that within a marriage. Perhaps the toughest assignment in a man's life is to take his wife's hand in his and say, "We're broke." It's not easy to accept, but it's much, much harder to say. But that simple, flat, honest statement is the beginning of the long road back to a stable economic reality. As long as either partner tries to pretend that there are no problems, that life can go on as it has been, the family will live in a position which is at odds with reality and which is therefore untenable. Honesty with each other is a necessary prerequisite to honesty with the outside world.

When there are children in the family, some of the communication has to be with them. They should not be loaded with worrisome details, but they need to understand the general outline of the reality the family is facing.

As the condition of our business gradually became public knowledge—and there are few secrets that can be kept
in a rural community—our children had to field questions
from friends at school. One day, Geoffrey, our nine-year-
old, came into the house.

"Dad," he asked, sounding extra casual, "is our company going broke?"

"Why?" Cam asked.

"Well, because Grant told me it was folding up."

"He's right, Geoff," Cam replied.

"What does that mean?"

Cam's policy of honesty led him to explain carefully but
simply to Geoff the way in which cattle-market conditions
and a killing August frost on our crops had worked together to bring the company to a position where it was
unable to repay its obligations without selling all of its
machinery and other assets.

In this day, it isn't easy to say to children, "We just can't
afford it," but that year we had to tell our children just that;
not only about such things as the Christmas goodies in the
stores and catalogs, but about items far more basic, such as
winter overshoes.

We simply didn't have the money to outfit all eight feet,
and they all needed new boots. So we told the children
about the situation, and as a family we prayed about it.
Each child prayed for his or her own winter boots, some
giving specifications as to the type they would prefer. The
Lord answered first by delaying snow. In our Alberta winters, we usually have permanent snow by the first week of
November. That winter, no snow fell and stayed until
December 22. And by that time, we had received a small
check that covered the cost of on-sale overshoes for all
eight feet.

Not, mind you, the bush boots Geoffrey had requested.
Nor the high-heeled, side-zipped tall boots of Cammie's

dreams. But, for all the children, warm, felt-lined, and in-style boots. The children learned to accept the Lord's provision with thanksgiving. It was an experience in learning not to take the good, basic provisions for granted or to demand the supply of more than our needs.

Economic pressures create a need—and an opportunity—for a family to really pull together. When the going gets rough, it is all too easy for a couple to begin to blame one another, to point a finger and say, "If you had just—". That root of bitterness must not be allowed to develop within a marriage. Actually, it is the very essence of blasphemy, which is blaming instead of praising. The day you start to talk about your "bad luck" or "curse your stars" or feel angry in your heart at God or your mate, you are on dangerous ground.

"Two are better than one," wrote Solomon. "For if either of them falls, the one will lift up his companion. But woe to the one who falls when there is not another to lift him up" (Ec 4:9-10, NASB). In times of hardship, we have often prayed that the Lord would never let both of us go down together. If one of us is finding that his faith and trust in God's provision is wavering, and his grip on the truth that "God causes all things to work together for good to those who love God" (Ro 8:28, NASB) slackening off, then the other's prayers and encouragement buoy up the sinking partner. That's one of God's good purposes in Christian marriage. Each partner has the privilege of ministering to the other's needs. Pity all the Jobs whose wives leave them without spiritual support in their time of economic adversity!

Hard times are times to read the Word of God together, daily, and discuss it. One of the really wonderful things about our hardest months was that, with the collapse of the farming company, Cam suddenly had some extra time in his days: time to read the Word, time to talk with me over that second cup of tea after supper, time to pray—at length—together. The message that came through, above all the others, to us was very simple and just this: that God is, indeed, our Father. And He gives only good gifts, even when the wrapping paper is not too attractive to our eyes.

I will long remember seeing my little mother after she and my father were involved in a serious car accident. She had been released from the hospital, but her face was still swollen and misshapen, and she had a huge orange and purple bruise over her eyes. Mother could not move without pain, but she sat stiffly on a straight kitchen chair as I prepared a meal. Speaking with difficulty, since it hurt her even to catch a breath, she said in her quiet way, "It doesn't feel good, darling, but it must be good." It was an articulation of the kind of holding-on faith that my parents lived out before their family. And it's the kind of faith that helped Cam and me to know that, back of the threatening clouds of economic reversals, shone the sun of God's loving-kindness.

As we tried to sort things out, Cam would say, "The Lord knows, and the Lord knows I don't know." That, too, was a statement of faith. Just that one fact—that our heavenly Father knew, both our situation and our real needs, material and spiritual—was enough to hold onto until we could begin to discern His "thoughts of . . . good" (Jer 29:11) expressed in our difficult circumstances.

Rooting out bitterness is one kind of emotional problem that you may need to handle with God's help in order to go on living in love in the face of financial hardship. Depression is another. The summer that we watched our business buckle under day by day, listening to the market reports as cattle prices slipped lower and lower, and then awakening one early August morning to find that there had been several degrees of frost which destroyed our immature crops, I fought depression by talking with my Lord.

"Lord," I prayed at one point, "none of this makes any sense to me at all. I only know one thing, and that is that *I love You.*" Declaring my love to God was a source of strength. But then, as things continued to get worse, I found myself praying another prayer. It ran something like this: "Lord, now it's all black and chaotic. I don't know anything at all now, except that *You love me.*" Now I had hit bedrock! I learned that no matter how we were tested, financially or physically or spiritually—and sometimes in all three ways at once—there was a bottom to it all. Underneath all our circumstances is the bedrock of the love of God in Christ Jesus, that love from which nothing can ever separate us.

When we got down past all the feelings, past all the external evidences, to the declared fact that by Jesus' sacrifice God has become our Father, and that a Father's heart is full of love toward His children and that by nature He is bound to give nothing but good gifts, including chastisement and correction, then the quiet joy of submitting to God's sovereign purposes became ours. And the love of God became a source, far greater than even our own great love for each other, on which we could draw as we learned to live on love.

Drawing on the unfailing source of love from God, a wife and family can be spiritually and emotionally supportive of a husband facing a business failure, the loss of a job, or a demotion. Psychiatrists classify such experiences as "potentially castrative." Certainly, it is very traumatic. The wife who finds herself worrying about her own feelings—about how hurt or deprived she is—is still immature in the art of loving. It is an act of mature love to feel for your husband at such a time, to put yourself into his uncomfortable boots. How would you feel if you had made decisions that brought hardship to your family? How would you feel if the goals you had set for yourself had been suddenly torn from your grasp? How would you face it if, by the criteria of the "Modern Money Myth," you were suddenly a failure?

The downbeat, depressed time of initial acceptance is not a time to analyze weaknesses, but to discover strengths, in each other. It is not a time for either partner to shrill, or even to whisper, "I told you so," but to say, and mean it, "I love you so." The key word in every conversation should be encouragement. It is not hard to destroy a person, especially someone who is hurt and bruised. At such a time, we need to remember the gentleness of Jesus who would not break a bruised reed. The wife who belittles a husband who is in the throes of a psychological trauma may make of him a "little husband," a broken person whom she will find it difficult to love and respect.

If a husband is out of work, he needs his wife's love and support to make him strong enough to go and look for another job. If he is facing loss, he needs encouragement to go on. He needs love, stated and shown, to help him rebuild his battered self-image. He needs to draw deeply on a wife's emotional support until he can reestablish his own emotional equilibrium.

Never, in any marriage, is there a time when loving support, deep sharing, and much prayer for a partner are more necessary. In easy times, it may be possible to assume each other's love. In hard times, that love needs to be stated and reiterated. Not some kind of phony, artificial love, but love based on the discovery of strengths in each other. The wife can commend the husband's integrity and appreciate his concern for his family, while the husband can praise the wife for her frugality and uncomplaining attitude. And love can thrive, for as Samuel Johnson pointed out, it is, after all, "a native of the rocks."

Later, as you pass through the experience together, you may both have insights that will help you to keep the

trauma from repeating itself. Under the guidance of the
Holy Spirit and with all of His dovelike tenderness, a wife
and a husband may minister to each other as they see
weaknesses develop under the strain, or as they come to
understand personal weakness that produced the strain in
the first place. It becomes a matter of spiritual and personal
survival to keep on "building up yourselves on your most
holy faith" (Jude 20).

As you commend each other's strengths and tenderly
minister to each other's weaknesses, you can prepare
yourselves to learn all that the Lord has for you in the
experience of hardship. I can remember a morning when
we were still trying to sort ourselves out after our debacle,
when we suddenly understood: *There are two ways to
respond to this experience. One is to withdraw, asking a
whining, 'Why?' and so shrivel in our souls. The other way
is to reach out both hands for the experience . . . to "press
against the pain" . . . to lean into the experience . . . and
thus to learn all we can about this aspect of the human
condition, and to grow.* We made up our minds that we
would grow—no matter how it hurt. And Cam and I have
found ourselves matured and quieted and corrected by the
things we have faced together.

Of course, the days of hardship need not be ones of
unbroken solemnity. In fact, heaven help the family who
cannot laugh at themselves, laugh at their situation. (We
do need to be careful here, for bitter laughter, laughter at
each other's expense, and derisive laughter are all destruc-
tive. It is only the gentle laughter of people seeing life
together, people who can see the ridiculousness of themselves or of their situation, that builds and helps.) The
merciful gift of being able to laugh at ourselves—laugh
with those we loved—was, for us, a healing agent. I remember when Cam decided to break the news of our
economic collapse to my parents. It wasn't easy for him.

"Dad," he said, as we lingered over second cups of coffee after breakfast that Thanksgiving, "I think you ought to know that we are in financial trouble."

My dad never flinched. He just smiled and said, "So, what's new?"

The laughter we shared together then was healing, as has been much of the laughter we have enjoyed together, both by ourselves and with friends and family.

Living on love means sharing the load. Sharing it in honest communication. Sharing it in recognition of individual strengths and honest acknowledgment of one another's failures. Sharing it in the assessment of lessons learned and new understandings gained. It also means sharing in the actual solution to the problem. It is not just enough to be honest with each other and then fold your hands and stare at the ceiling, waiting for a handout from the sky. God just does not work in that way. In fact, the New Testament is explicit about the necessity for "working with . . . [our] hands the thing which is good" (Eph 4:28).

Let me share with you a letter my mother wrote to her four children when she explained the terms of my grandfather's will. It tells a story of how a whole family shared the load.

Grandpa and Grandma Woods were very hard working people with simple tastes and a contentment with their lot in life—always grateful to the Lord for His provision for them and their three children. Our home was furnished with plain, even rugged furniture, a few chintz cushions for the seats of the hardwood chairs being the only upholstery we knew. As we grew up and visited in the homes of our friends, we children began to see the new overstuffed Chesterfield suites which were really quite new on the market and we began to pester our parents for more elaborate things. Grandpa put a proposition to us: If we would help them save $1,000 as a cushion for emergencies first, they would then add some better furniture to our home. I would have been about ten or eleven years old, and my brothers were younger, so you realize the only way we could help was by not asking for things we didn't need.

We watched the bank account grow with real interest and did reach our goal. However, about the same time as we reached that goal, Grandpa lost his job with Canadian Pacific Railways because of the economic crash in 1929. He was able to get enough work that the emergency fund was not depleted but even we children understood that luxuries were out. Then one day there was no more work to be obtained and Grandpa decided to try creating his own job. With the $1,000 he set up in business and God honored and prospered far beyond any expectation so that he was able to support and educate his family and provide jobs for his two sons when jobs were very difficult for young men to find. Grandpa never went into debt for anything either in business or in the home. If there was not cash to pay for things, we did without, but we never lacked any of the necessities of life and Grandpa was never on "relief" or welfare as we know it now. As long as we lived at home there was no new furniture but later, when things improved after the Second World War, Grandpa and Grandma did enjoy comforts which we today think are necessities.

Grandpa was generous in his giving to the Lord's work, and I cannot tell you how grateful I am to the Lord and to Grandpa and Grandma, not merely for the money in the estate, but for the godly heritage they have given us—the example of frugal living combined with a deep desire to obey God's Word at any cost.

There may, of course, be times when it is necessary for a Christian family to accept the goodness of the state in welfare or unemployment insurance. Sometimes there is no other choice. But as people of God we should do everything in our power to find ways to earn the bread we eat and to repay the debts we have incurred.

Obviously, when facing a cut in income, a job loss, a disability, or a business failure, the big problem is money. How do we find enough for day-to-day needs and, in many cases, enough to begin to pay back debts? Job-hunting is unpleasant in the best of times, but it is doubly difficult when a person is feeling crushed and damaged in self-esteem. But finding something to do to meet immediate needs is probably the biggest single step toward recovery. It may mean taking a job far beneath what you deem to be your level of ability. It may mean assessing the mutual job-finding resources of your family, with several members finding part-time work to help out. It may be that the wife will have to take a job for a while if, for example, her skills are more readily marketable than her husband's. And if that should happen, then the man must do his share by taking on the housework and meal-making duties. Actually, it can turn into a good change of pace for both parties.

When we were so hard pressed, the job available was teaching half-day high school French in a nearby town. Well, that ruled out Cam. Although he is a teacher with a great deal of experience, French is not one of his fields. Besides, he was still very much involved in marketing company assets and also doing the paperwork to try to wind down the company operation. So I took the job. I had not taught French for many years, but I did have the necessary university preparation.

I crammed all morning and taught all afternoon. And Cam kept house, did the wash, and made the meals. In about three months I was tired of teaching, and Cam was tired of housekeeping. But by that time he had completed much of the business, restored himself psychologically to a large extent, and was ready to take on a full-time teaching job made available by another teacher taking a maternity leave. Cam had been able to look after our two preschoolers in the afternoons while I taught until he began full-time teaching; now the children, too, became involved in "sharing the load." Grandma and Grandpa Hancock graciously undertook to care for Heather Ruth and Mitchell. When the children found it hard to change their play patterns and pack up for the daily drive to town, I would simply explain to them, "We're all helping each other just now. Grandma and Grandpa are helping by looking after you. Mummy is helping by teaching, and you can help by getting on your coats and not complaining!" And help they did, in just that way.

And so our hard winter unraveled itself into spring, with our clothes and groceries and gas being paid for as we went along. But had there been no teaching jobs available in our area, we would have sought other alternatives. Cam was offered a number of other jobs, and he gave each offer serious consideration. For, when economic reversal hits, one cannot consider oneself "above" any type of employment, regardless of previous training or job status. We knew that we would take work—any kind of work—to prevent ourselves from going further backward. And at the same time, we pruned our already lean life-style to fit within our reduced budget.

As you honestly face your problem and intelligently and prayerfully devise strategies for coping, you will find that the dark clouds will begin to rift just a little. And then, occasionally, a ray of sunshine will stray through. Finally, the clouds, still all piled up around you, will part enough so that you can see—as we did—that behind the clouds there is still a blue sky, and the sun is still in its place. God is there. Trust Him patiently, day by day. You may claim His promises for provision of your needs as you do your part in rehabilitating your finances. Meanwhile, you can face the challenge of learning to live—practically—on love.

# 5

# STOP THE MERRY-GO-ROUND

I spill the little plastic cards out across my desk here beside my typewriter: Texaco, Gulf, Woodward's, Eaton's, and Simpson's, every one of them attractively embossed with our very own names. At one time, they were my passports to sophisticated shopping. Today, they are just souvenirs of a bygone era in our life, an era when we bought by the line, "Want it? Charge it!" It was an era when it gave me a feeling of being "in" to pass my charge card across the counter and watch the cashier ratchet it through her little machine. All so clean and neat and painless.

But now when the lady at the cash register asks, "Charge?" in that pleasant, "You *do* belong, don't you?" sort of way, I shake my head firmly. "No. Cash." I give her my money and I double-check my change, and when I get home from shopping I know exactly how much I have spent, and I haven't bought one more thing than I actually had the money for.

Cam and I grew up in the "good old days" when credit was the magic key that unlocked all the goodies that adults could have. By means of credit, any young couple could virtually start living at the level their parents had achieved after many years of building a home. So, in the early days of our marriage, we applied for credit cards—and received them—by the bundle. (That was before the days of Chargex and Mastercharge, but apart from the bulkiness of one's wallet, the feeling was just the same.) We were cautious with those cards. One of the first uses we made of them was to outfit our home with simple, basic furniture. We were certainly not spendthrift, for we bought everything on sale and chose the least expensive things of reasonable quality that we could find. Thinking back on the sum total of our expenditures, the figure seems ludicrously small. The department store delivered the furniture to our village home, and the monthly statements began to arrive in our mailbox. They were really no problem since we were both earning paychecks. Nonetheless, I remember the feeling of discouragement when, month after month, we made our $50 payments, and the balance we still owed seemed to go down so painfully slowly. It was my first taste of the fact that it was much easier to charge than to pay.

We quit charging, all at once, when we decided to go back to the university together. We started to save instead. And the interest, instead of adding onto a balance payable account, started to be added to our credit balance in our savings account. We banked all of my check each month, and lived and made our payments from Cam's. There were student loans available in those days, as there are now. But somehow, it wasn't very attractive for us to go into debt for our education. So we came out of the university after lean years, debt free and with enough money left over to make a down payment on a car, buy a little nine by twelve foot tent (still our basic camping equipment), and make a memorable cross-Canada camping trip.

But then we entered consumer life in earnest. Cam was principal of a school. His income was about the same as our combined salaries had been prior to our return to the university. I was expecting our first child and had time to turn the pages of the fat catalogs which, for people in rural areas like ours, served as department stores. And, with my shiny new credit cards, I was able to charge the things we needed. I'm sure that everything I bought was quite legitimate and defensible. I know I never shopped frivolously. But I remember the sudden shock and panic that struck me when, after the delight of numbers of little parcels arriving in the mail, the statements followed. I could hardly imagine that the "few little things" I had bought had pushed the balance on our two accounts to a combined $300. The other shock came over the next few months. Do you know how long it takes to reduce a balance of $300 at the minimum monthly payment of $12? Forever. At least, it seems that long. Especially if you happen to add a thing or two to that account as you go along.

I was learning that the exciting consumer concept of revolving credit was a merry-go-round with the music stuck in an endless, mindless ditty of "buy now, and pay and pay and pay." It was a merry-go-round that never had to stop at all. And every ad I read, every page of every catalog, every visit to the department stores in the city, and every mailing "To preferred credit customers" was designed to flatter me with the idea that somehow I was a notch above the rest of the world because I held a silver and blue or yellow and white or red and pink credit card for a given store. I was a member of the club.

Then we went farming. And when big spending times of the year came around—like snowsuit time or Christmas— and there simply was no money because the grain was still not marketed, the charge cards came in handy again. I could rattle off those tempting numbers and, after dictating my order, say nonchalantly, "Just charge it to our account." I knew my numbers by heart. And I was treated

with the deference given to regular charge customers. The
balances began to build up again.

Worst of all, the monthly statements had a way of coming out to coincide with the time when most average
people were bringing home their paychecks. But we had
no paycheck. Just those big, tantalizing lump sums that
came with shipping a load of pigs or selling a bin of
grain—those big checks that all seemed to be paid out to
the men who had delivered our gas, stockpiled our fer-
tilizer, or sold us seed. It was hard to scratch up enough, on
a month to month basis, to pay even the minimum payments on those charge accounts. And if there's one thing I
cannot face, it's a dunner. "We hope that your failure to
make a payment last month was an oversight. However,
terms of our credit agreement with you stipulate that if we
do not receive your payment of _____ by
_____, we shall _____." Those notes
devastated me. Not that we were defaulting in any long-
term way. As soon as there was money, we paid the back
payment and one or two in advance. We simply limped
from lump to lump. And between times, I would find
myself having to charge something or other, pushing up
that balance once again.

It finally dawned on me that the whole principle of the
revolving credit system was that you should never get a
balance paid off. You should always have a balance, pay
interest on it, pay off some and add on some. And about the
same time, it dawned on me that it was those monthly
accounts that made me most unhappy and most discontent. They were the things that precipitated those "Why
can't we live like normal people?" discussions with Cam
which cheered him so. Combining with fiendish regular-
ity with my monthly "down"—those days when I felt a bit
mad at the world in general—those bills made month ends
bluer than any Midol ad ever pictured.

One year I finally made the big decision: there was no way that I was going to charge one thing for Christmas. Not one little thing. Cam and I liked to have great Christmas gifts for the kids. But when we noticed that we were still paying for one Christmas in November of the following year, we made our decision firm. "No matter how little we can buy, we're going to pay cash for Christmas gifts this year." Now, that may sound only reasonable to you, but for us it was a new departure, a new beginning. We paid cash for Christmas, trimming the gift list, withdrawing from drawing names, and shopping as thriftily as we could. And on that Christmas Day, every gift that was opened was prepaid. The only day nicer than December 25 was January 25, when there were no additional charges on those revolving accounts of ours. And February 25. And March 25. Less pressure, less depression, fewer arguments.

That experiment prepared us to take action when, several years later, we found that our company was completely broke. We took what little money we had in the bank and paid all of our charge accounts: gas accounts, department store accounts, and grocery account. It left us flat broke. But from that day we decided that either the Lord would supply us with cash or we would not buy. That applied right down to the next loaf of bread we needed for school lunches. We learned to pray, "Give us this day our daily bread." And He did. There was often very little extra. Cam used to say, "You know, our cupboards would make Mother Hubbard's look like a supermarket." But there was always enough—for that day, at least.

I remember in particular a week when all our stocks were at an all-time low. But we had no money. None at all. So we took our request to the Lord in prayer. The last day of the week, the mail contained two small checks: one a reprint fee for an article of mine, the other a small overpayment refund for Cam. The total was no staggering amount, but we went shopping. We shopped with all the joy I used to know as a little girl with a dime to spend in Woolworth's. We shopped selectively. We picked things up, adding up the total in our heads as we went, and then pushed the cart back and put some of the things back on the shelves. And when we went home, we had all that we needed. Plus joy and gratitude.

The greatest delight, besides that of having no more month-end pressures when month ends brought so little of anything else, was the pleasure of being freed from the need to buy. I could look at one of those ads reading, "Go Ahead! Charge It!" and feel more nausea than desire. I had the happy feeling that month by month, despite inflation, I was at least not having to pay those scarcely perceptible little service charges and exorbitant 18½ percent interest rates that are normal on credit-card accounts.

I noticed something else, too. Without those credit cards in my purse, I was free to shop. I mean, really shop. I didn't have to go to the stores where I was a gilt-edged, card-carrying member. I could go anywhere for the best values. I noticed it most of all when buying gas. As long as I had a particular company's card in my purse, all I looked for was a service station sporting the right color and shape of sign, and wheeled in for gas. Without those little bits of plastic, I read, instead, the price-per-gallon signs, and bought where the price was right.

Getting off the credit merry-go-round was just part of our overall "face the facts" policy. Not that using a charge card is dishonest, of course. But allowing yourself to buy things you cannot afford today, in the hope that you will be able to afford them—plus interest—next month, is living a myth. So is it when you think that buying things in easy monthly payments is really easy. It's not. Without those plastic crutches, I could look at our bank balance and decide whether I could afford to buy or not. Some years, it has been mostly not. And yet, the goodness of the Lord's provision is unforgettable.

If you are on the credit-card trip and want to get off, let me give you a few tips. First of all, in order to get the charge accounts paid, you will have to impose a period of several months of real austerity on yourself, buying only absolute necessities like groceries. If you have a regular income, budget to pay off the accounts in an orderly way as fast as you can. And put nothing—but nothing—more on that account. "I can hardly wait," a friend of mine told me. "In a couple of months, we should have all our accounts paid off. Then we're going to only buy with cash." And then she went to the city with her charge cards in her purse. The temptation was too much as she browsed in the big stores. "It all only came to $75," she told me as she showed me her purchases. "I just charged it." Six months later we each drained a Coke as we chatted. "That miserable charge account is right up there again," she sighed. "And it all started that time I charged those clothes."

The only way to stop the merry-go-round is to put those credit cards in some safe and nonpilferable place— anywhere but your purse. If you do not want to destroy them yet, store them in an envelope, deep in a file, or, better yet, in your safety deposit box. That will make them hard to grab when your fingers get the dial-an-order itch. If you must make purchases while you are trying to reduce your charge accounts, pay cash. And chisel away at the balances you owe as fast as you can. Then, when the accounts are down to a zero balance and you get that lovely letter, reading, "We are pleased with the excellent way in which you have handled your credit. Please feel free to use your credit card at any time"—and the follow-up one which tells you what a valued customer you are and how they yearn to punch your computer card just once more— forget it! It's not real love.

Now, at last, you can begin to live in the real world. And despite all the talk of unlimited credit, despite the idea that floated around us like pretty bubbles all the time we were growing up—that money was not really necessary as long as credit existed—everyone in the Western world from government to individuals has got to face reentry into the reality of economics: for any goods received, value must be given. And the easiest, surest, most direct way to be sure that you can give value for goods received is to pay as you go. It's so old-fashioned that it is avant-garde. Just ask the mayor of New York City.

Living in this real world, you will have to exercise restraint. Nobody else is going to restrain you. But with the help of the Lord, as you develop a contented and a quiet heart, you will learn how to distinguish between wants and needs, something our merchandising world does not really want you to know. "My God shall supply all your needs," is our Lord's promise, and it is guaranteed "according to his riches in glory by Christ Jesus" (Phil 4:19). But nowhere, not anywhere, does the Lord invite us to help ourselves to everything we want. In fact, we are solemnly warned against "the lust of the flesh, and the lust of the eyes, and the pride of life" (1 Jn 2:16). Try analyzing the advertising techniques used in magazines and newspapers by those three phrases, and you will find that the world is geared to pandering to those three tastes. The Christian should know another set of desires that lifts him above the need to be an insatiable consumer.

I have found that one way to separate needs from wants is to make a list of things I would like to have, the things that are sort of pressing in on me. And then I prayerfully stroke out the things that are just wants. Needs are basic: clothes suitable to the climate in which we live, warm and adequate housing, food for our families, some mode of transportation. Wants are peripheral. And in a day of

affluent Christianity in the Western world, it is well to
remind ourselves that God never promised that He would
supply warm clothing in the form of mink jackets,
adequate housing in the form of prestige-loaded split-
levels, good food in the form of shrimp cocktails, or transportation in the form of top-of-the-line cars. But we can be
confident that He will supply our needs.

Perhaps another way to separate needs from wants
would be to ask about any purchase, "Is this an item I
might want to put in a garage sale in a few short years?" An
unsigned editorial in *Christianity Today*, entitled, "How
Not to Have a Garage Sale," comments:

> The current popularity of the garage sale shows how
> quickly we outgrow "needs." That aquarium and electric
> juicer and exercise bike that we absolutely had to have soon
> turned into white elephants. We can't bear to throw them
> out, and thus concede that we didn't need them after all, so
> we seek to sell them. If we can get a little something for
> them we'll feel less uncomfortable about our mistakes. And
> besides, we'll have something to apply toward our new-
> found needs.

> Alas, the cycle is not easy to break in our affluent society. A
> place to start is to resist impulse buying, even as "50%
> Off!" Christians particularly should set the example by
> concentrating their spending on things of more lasting
> value.[1]

I have been talking about getting off the endless merry-
go-round of credit for consumable items. There are, of
course, other kinds of completely legitimate credit which I
am sure God intends for Christians to use wisely and well.
Very few families could have a home if they had to pay
cash for it. Very few could start a business. And most
would not even be able to drive a car. Christian thinkers
have drawn a distinction between borrowing for consum-

able items (debt) and borrowing for capital items (investment). This difference is set forth memorably in Robert Schuller's account of how his banker explained to him the meaning of debt:

> When you borrow money for coal you are going into debt. The coal will be burned. When it is gone, if you are unable to pay your loan, there is nothing you can sell to pay us back. When you borrow money for coal, or food, or the light bill, or the water bill, you are spending money that is gone forever. This is real debt.

But, the banker went on to explain:

> If you want to borrow money to buy a car or a house, we will lend you money. Then you are not going into debt; you are going into the investment business. . . . If you borrow money to buy a store and you borrow money for salable goods to put on the shelves, you are not in debt. You are in business.[2]

Yet, here again, a clear head, an open Bible, a good banker, and a clear line of communication between you and your mate are necessary to be sure that you are using credit instead of it using you. In our farming company, the money we borrowed was very legitimate and used for the purposes of production. Yet, we still borrowed ourselves into very serious economic problems. An article in Changing Times, The Kiplinger Magazine, suggests "one safety rule is never to owe more at any one time than you can repay within 12 months at your current rate of payments," making, of course, exceptions for large, long-term loans such as those for homes.[3] Another rule of thumb would be never to borrow more than you have fixed assets to cover. Thus, if you found yourself unable to meet current obligations, you would be able to sell assets and cover your indebtedness.

Friends of ours recently recounted to us that when their

insurance agent came to review their coverage, they decided to have him help them draw up a net worth statement. They listed all of their assets in one column, and
totaled them; all of their liabilities were listed in a second
column and totaled. When the insurance man subtracted
the total liabilities from their total assets, he looked up at
them, obviously surprised. They had a substantial surplus
of assets over liabilities. "You know," the insurance
salesman told them, "there are very few couples today who
have a positive net worth. When I work this out for most
people, we find they actually owe more than they own."

Another problem remains to be discussed in this credit-
abundant society. What about credit debts which you have
at the moment that your business goes sour? Or you lose
your job? Or illness destroys your earning power while
adding burdens?

A Christian cannot just walk away from debt. His word is
pledged, and he must acknowledge his obligations. But,
"if you have nothing with which to pay, why should he
take your bed from under you?" (Pr 22:27, NASB). To
avoid such an unpleasant outcome, the best route is simply
to be honest and open. Go to your creditors personally, or
write them a letter. Explain the situation and ask for time
in which to reorganize your finances. Suggest a time when
you will be able to begin to reduce the debt, if that time can
be foreseen. Let them know your fiscal condition, and
assure them that you are serious about repaying the obligation. If you are straightforward and honest, if you have
pared down your life-style to an extremely modest standard so that you are credible, if you continue to keep in
touch and make even token payments of good faith, then
your creditors will be remarkably patient as you attempt to
get your business affairs straightened out.

I once worked as a typist in collection agencies. In one
office, I typed envelopes while at ten or twelve desks in the

same large room ten or twelve men sat and dialed persons whose debts were considered "bad" and had been turned over to them for collection. The men yelled and threatened and bullied, and I felt the horror of how it must feel to be at the other end of such a call. But creditors do not like turning accounts over to collection agencies, since they lose a percentage of every payment collected. Despite financial problems, we have found that honesty with our creditors, restraint in our personal living, and systematic planning for repayment of staggering debts have resulted in fair and courteous treatment from those to whom we have owed money. We rejected bankruptcy as a means of avoiding debt obligations, even though our debts had been incurred by a limited company. And, through the goodness of the Lord and the patience of our creditors, we expect to be able to pay back "the uttermost farthing" (Mt 5:26).

On our honeymoon, Cam and I went to the Pacific National Exhibition ground with some friends in Vancouver. We went through the exhilaration and terror of the enormous roller coaster, tumbled on the trampolines, and took some other rides. And then we all went out together for Alka-Seltzer to settle our stomachs.

That is sort of the way we feel right now. We have gotten off the merry-go-round. And though we're still feeling just a little bit sick, we are looking forward to full recovery.

# 6

# BASIC NEEDS I: SHARING THE GOOD THINGS

One of our greatest adventures started on the day that a young missionary couple with two small children stayed overnight with us while they were traveling through our area. We had missed their meeting at our church, so they gave us a "private screening" of their slides of France, shared with us some of the highs and lows of trying to share the Good News in a country that just does not seem all that interested, and told us their own personal stories of God's good work in their lives. The next morning, as Cam helped Ken pack things into their car, he found himself groping for words. We wanted to share in the work of these new friends, but we had very little ourselves. "Ken," Cam said, "I just wish I could promise you more. But we will pledge $5 a month toward your support." We could offer so little that it was almost embarrassing.

Others, all across the United States and Canada, pledged their little bits. And Ken and Bernice Frenzel went back to their work in France with the Bible Christian Union. They were good communicators, and we received regular circular letters, postmarked in France, naming specific prayer requests and reasons for praise. We learned about the people to whom they were having a witness, and we prayed specifically for those contacts. One young lady, a university student, was showing an interest in the Word, one of the letters told us. We prayed. And sent our little month-by-month remittance to mission headquarters.

And then one day we received a surprise letter. It was a personal note in Ken's crisp script. "A young lady to whom we have been explaining the gospel, a university student, would like to spend a month or so this summer in the home of a North American family. Would you be able to welcome her into your home?"

Just at that moment, we were not just sure where we would be living by summertime, the only prospect being the small square old house I have already described. It was going to be small for our family. Wherever would we put one more? Besides, we didn't know a thing about the girl. How could we be sure we could live with her under our eaves for a month? How could we be sure that she could stand us for that long? But, on the other hand, suppose we were Ken and Bernice, hoping for a further Christian witness to an openhearted young person? We could give only one answer, and it went something like this:

> DEAR KEN and BERNICE,
>
> Of course your friend may come and stay with us—as long as she is able to survive in chaotic conditions. We think we will probably have to move in May, and so may not even be fully settled. But if she is willing to cope with family living in close quarters, we will be glad to have her.
>
> CAM and MAXINE

Our next communication came directly from the young lady. I still have that letter:

> It is thoughtful of you to be willing to welcome me this summer. I look forward to knowing you and your family

according to what Ken and Bernice Frenzel told me about
your way of life.

It will be a pleasure for me to help you—especially if you
are expecting to move.

Don't worry about what you call "a chaotic kind of household." I think it is the same thing at home.

I would rather come early in Summer than at the end of the
July because some of the Travel Agencies in Paris may need
me to guide Tourists as I had succeeded in their exams.

Would the dates fit you? I do not wish to disturb you.

I am going now to plan my journey!

SINCERELY,

BETTY LACASSAGNE

As summer drew closer, we received another letter telling
the exact time of Betty's arrival, together with a passport-
type photograph of her. We studied the photograph, trying
to imagine the personality that would go with that sweet
yet sophisticated face under a mop of curly hair. We ar-
ranged for my parents to meet her plane at the Edmonton
International Airport and bring her halfway to our country
home.

And we prayed. By then, we had shoehorned ourselves
into our new small home, and we wondered how we
would manage with one more adult. Then came the Sunday afternoon when we met her: a pretty, tiny French girl,
speaking English with little more facility than I spoke
French, which meant that we would often meet about
halfway in communications.

That day began one of the richest and happiest months
of our lives, and one of the shortest. Betty was an immediate favorite with the children. In return for her board
and room, she treated us to French-cooked meals each day;

she sewed doll clothes for the girls' dolls and made me an up-to-the-minute Parisian-style skirt. And we talked— Cam and Betty and I—for hours about life in our two countries, about literature, about education, and about salvation through faith in the Lord Jesus Christ. While she was in our home, Betty was reading a French translation of John Stott's *Basic Christianity*, given to her before her trip by Ken and Bernice. We found that our missionary friends had done a very thorough job of teaching her the underlying doctrines of evangelical Christianity. Until she had begun discussions with them, she had considered herself an agnostic, "with nothing firm to stand on, only an endless marsh of ideas." Now she was reading her Bible and seriously considering becoming a confessing Christian.

One day, Betty was very upset. She had read Stott's chapter on the sinfulness of man, and was under deep conviction. "I did not know I was so terrible a person!" she exclaimed. "I could not sleep to think about it."

The next day her face was aglow as she came down from the upstairs bedroom where she slept. "I have made my decision. I will receive Christ as my Lord and Saviour. I have seen in your home that this will affect all of life. But I was at first afraid it would make one very grave and solemn." We laughed together. Our home was anything but solemn. "I have seen from your family what Ken and Bernice explained from the Bible. There is no difference for you between religion and life; it is all of one piece. And so it shall be for me."

When the day came to say good-bye to Betty, the children sobbed as the plane lifted off the runway. It was hard for all of us to part with one who had become so intrinsically united with our family in that tiny month. But our parting was made easier in knowing the joy she would bring to Ken and Bernice back in her hometown in France.

We stood on the observation deck until we could no longer see the plane, realizing, as we did so that because of our little $5-a-month investment, we had experienced the joy of sharing in our friends' overseas ministry. Our children had experienced a touch with another culture, I had practiced my French, our home and our lives had been enriched, and we had been privileged to watch God move in a life. Talk about dividends!

No matter how hard pressed we have been, we have been aware that one of our first and most basic needs was the need to give. "I just can't afford to give," some people sigh. But the real fact of the matter is that none of us can afford not to give. As believers in and disciples of the Lord Jesus Christ, we need to give or we will fail to know the fullness of God's goodness to us, and shrivel spiritually. As C. S. Lewis puts it:

> Charity—giving to the poor—is an essential part of Christian morality. . . . If anyone thinks that . . . you can stop giving then he has parted company with all Christian morality. . . . If our charities do not at all pinch or hamper us, I should say they are too small.[1]

Giving is a basic need for the believer. And, on our list of priorities, it must supersede all other needs. Many, many have found that when they have tried to save a little at the end of each month for giving, they have nothing to give. But, on the other hand, when they set aside their gifts first, and then deal with the other necessities, there is somehow always enough to go around.

The fact that giving is a basic need of all believers is stressed over and over in the New Testament. To His penniless disciples, Jesus turned over the responsibility of feeding a huge, hungry crowd. "Give ye them to eat" (Mt 14:16). The disciples were stunned when they did the mental calculations and felt their empty purses. They learned that, in order to fulfill their Lord's command, they would have to rely on their Lord's resources.

Paul enlarged on the theme of openhanded giving initiated by Christ. He invited the Philippian Christians to give, not as a response to his needs, but because giving produces lasting spiritual benefit in the lives of the givers (see Phil 4:10-20).

Of course, giving is not a novel theme in the New Testament. It is simply an enlargement of a theme already developed throughout the Old Testament. Because God is love, those throughout history who have understood, however dimly, His revelation of Himself, have understood the obligation of sharing the good things of life. The tradition of giving can be verbally traced as far back as to Job who, in defending his righteous conduct, recounts his acts of charity thus:

> If I have kept the poor from their desire,
> Or have caused the eyes of the widow to fail,
> Or have eaten my morsel alone,
> And the orphan has not shared it. . . .
> If I have seen anyone perish for lack of clothing, . . .
> And if he has not been warmed with the fleece of my sheep. . . .
> Let my shoulder fall from the socket,
> And my arm be broken off at the elbow.
>
> JOB 31:16-22 (NASB)

Job explains that he has been moved to such acts by the fear of the Lord. The New Testament believer who claims to be motivated by love should surely not do less.

Giving is a need. Not only because there are physical needs which must be met by our giving—and never have there been more than those which surround us and clamor for our attention today—but because in giving we learn something of the "grace of our Lord Jesus Christ, that, though He was rich, yet for your sake He became poor" (2 Co 8:9, NASB). In giving, in sharing, we learn a little of what it is to be like Christ. In sharing His tears and His heartache for the spiritual, physical, and intellectual needs of His creatures, and in doing something concrete to help meet those needs, we begin to bear a family resemblance to the One whom we call Father, who is the Giver of "every good gift and every perfect gift" (Ja 1:17).

Giving is a need, too, because it somehow clears a channel through which we can receive God's provision for us. Jesus made it clear that if we do not forgive others, we block out God's forgiveness to us. It is not that our unforgiving spirit makes God unable to forgive. It is that in being unforgiving, we become unable to receive His forgiveness. Similarly, when we fail to give to others, we block the channel by which God makes His goodness available to us. This is made clear in the unforgettable passage in Malachi in which God invites His people, "Bring ye all the tithes into the storehouse, . . . and prove [test] me now herewith, saith the LORD of hosts, if I will not open you the windows of heaven, and pour you out a blessing, that there shall not be room enough to receive it" (Mal 3:10).

Of course we have to be careful that we do not lock ourselves into a vicious, and un-Christian, circle of "giving to get." Yet, at the same time, we can understand that giving—even out of the extremes of poverty—is taught throughout Scripture as a means for opening ourselves to the Lord's goodness. If we are to come to God and request that He meet our material needs as He has promised, then we must be sure that we are also concerning ourselves with and expending ourselves on the needs of others.

Giving—and especially giving when we ourselves are needy—is an exercise of faith, a spiritual act. Of course, it cannot be done foolishly. It cannot be done in an attempt to lever God into doing something for us. A young fellow in our young adult Sunday school class shared with us a lesson he had learned about God's sovereignty. A Bible school student, he had very much wanted to go to the Inter-Varsity Christian Fellowship Urbana missionary conference one Christmas. He had the necessary $100. "But," he reasoned, "if I were to give that money to the Lord, maybe He would give me double that much. Or even multiply it tenfold." So, with visions of dollar signs dancing in his head, Bill put his $100 on the offering plate. He did not go to Urbana. The Lord had entrusted to him the amount needed for that trip, and it was an act of poor stewardship to do otherwise with it. Thus, we do not give away the money the Lord has given us for a mortgage payment and expect to get double the amount in the mail the next day. We budget our income and discipline ourselves to give in accordance with three clear New Testament principles:

1. *Motivation:* At a banquet head table, I sat next to the minister of a church which was slowly dying of financial strangulation. "Our people just don't give like yours do," he told me. "What is the secret of your church?" He knew that our church, with only about forty-five members and about as many regular nonmembers attending, was able to support a full-time resident minister and a church-expansion project, and still give generously to missions. "How do you do it?"

"It's just this," I told him. "Our people are taught from the Scripture that they must give their whole selves to the Lord. Having done that, generous giving is a by-product of discipleship. If you give your congregation a teaching ministry that explains and requires the commitment of the whole life to the lordship of Jesus Christ, giving will just naturally follow."

He sighed. It was not a message his congregation would

find very acceptable, he knew. And meanwhile, he had his annual budget to pare into balance.

The motivation of all truly Christian giving is loving self-giving. The Macedonian Christians whom Paul so warmly commended to the Corinthians epitomized such giving:

> In a great ordeal of affliction their abundance of joy and their deep poverty overflowed in the wealth of their liberality. For . . . according to their ability, and beyond their ability they gave of their own accord, . . . and this, not as we had expected, but they first gave themselves to the Lord (2 Co 8:2-5, NASB).

So then, neither do we give to get, nor do we give because God is personally in need of our gifts. This idea is hooted at in a number of passages of Scripture. Why, God has all riches. All power is His. He owns "the cattle upon a thousand hills" (Ps 50:10). (And cattlemen may smile ruefully some days and think, *And He's welcome to them!*) We do not give because we have a God who needs to be plastered with gold leaf. We give because our living and eternal God deigns to use our resources to accomplish His work. We give because in giving we grow. We give because we have given our whole lives to the Lord. We give because it is the natural, glad response of love and thanksgiving to God's goodness to us.

There have been times when we have been able to give a good deal. And times when we have had little to give. There have been times when we could give with the delight of skimming a cup of cream off the milk of our lives. And there have been times when the milk was so thin it was blue, and we offered from the skim milk. We have always known that God was pleased to accept and bless our gifts, whether they came from our prosperity or from our adversity.

2. *Measure:* How much to give? Evangelical churches, and many orthodox traditional churches, have long taught the principle of the tithe. Neoorthodox and modern liberal churches eschew such teaching as smacking of legalism. "Do you know," I once heard a little elderly lady tell a circle of church women around her, "I have gotten to know some people who go to the ——————— Church." Her voice fell to a scandalized whisper. "And do you know? They actually *tithe.*" The women around clucked their tongues in disbelief, and went back to planning their fund-raising tea and bazaar.

If the tithe was for the Old Testament, while the New Testament—as some would tell us—does away with such legalism, we should remember that the New Testament standard would then be much, much higher. For Jesus fulfilled the whole Law in Himself and set the standard of total giving. Most people, if they really saw how high Christ's standard is, would probably retreat to the safety and tidiness of the tithe.

I want to recommend the tithe as a basic first step toward systematic giving. An interesting principle in the Word of God is this: the tithe was first mentioned, not at the giving of the Mosaic Law, but long before. (Its concept lies behind the teaching of Heb 7.) The first mention of tithing is with Abraham. And Abraham, while the physical progenitor of the Jewish nation, is the spiritual father of all who receive salvation by faith (as Paul delineates in Ro 4). This great giant of faith who was saved, not by the keeping of the Law, but by "grace . . . through faith" (Eph 2:8) alone, this spiritual ancestor of ours, Abraham, tithed. The evidence is clear. If Abraham tithed, not because tithing was a law, nor because it in some way helped to buy acceptance with God, but because it was a principle of giving he had been taught either by tradition or by God Himself, then those of us who live the life of faith in the grace of God could well follow his example.

Jacob, too, tithed. He tithed in a simple, matter-of-fact business transaction: "If God will be with me and will keep me on this journey . . . and will give me food to eat and garments to wear, and I return to my father's house in safety, then the LORD will be my God . . . and of all that Thou dost give me I will surely give a tenth to Thee" (Gen 28:20-22, NASB). That does not sound quite so lofty as Abraham's worship and love-motivated gift to Melchizedek. But it does show that the principle of tithing is rooted not in a works' salvation, not in an obsolete law, but deeply in the tradition of men in personal relationship to an unseen but real God.

Later in the Old Testament, Malachi writes a dialogue between God and Israel in which God asks, "Will a man rob God? Yet ye have robbed me." Self-righteously, the people reply, "Wherein have we robbed thee?" And the Lord God's answer is simple and clear: "In tithes and offerings" (Mal 3:8).

It is completely compatible with Scripture to see the tithe as the basic unit of giving: first, because it is rooted in pre-Law relationships of man and God; second, because God considers that anything less is simple robbery of what is His; and third, because the principle is echoed in the New Testament in the principle of proportional giving. "Upon the first day of the week let every one of you lay by him in store, *as God hath prospered him*" (1 Co 16:2, itals. added). Whether the Lord has given us much or little, returning to Him 10 percent of that income is a way to be sure that our giving is proportional to our prosperity.

Tithing is the basic building block of giving. The phrase "tithes and offerings" has been interpreted to mean that over and above tithes are the gifts that can truly be called offerings. My parents, often hard pressed, used to say, "We don't feel that we're giving anything at all to the Lord when we put in our tithe. That just belongs to Him. It is His already. Giving starts where tithing leaves off." And I can remember an envelope on my parents' dresser—glimpsed, I suppose, when I could first read cursive handwriting— with the label: "Lord's Money." That envelope was the first thing attended to when the monthly earnings were brought in. Everything else came after that.

Giving, then, represents digging a bit deeper or reaching a bit higher. For some in extreme duress, the tithe may be absolutely all that can be returned to the Lord. For others, the tithe will be a small portion of what can be spared. For people who carry a heavy debt load, a matter of integrity is involved. After they have tithed, they must give primary attention to the repaying of contracted obligations. God cannot be honored by Christians who default on debts or postpone repayment in order to respond to some need. (And, by the way, that's just one more good reason to keep off the credit merry-go-round. If you don't have those monthly statements to pay, you may be able to cinch in your belt and give generously to a need that the Lord brings to your attention.) I find most challenging a concept of "needs limitation" in which Christian families accept a fixed figure at which they can live simply and modestly but without undue pressure. They adjust that figure to the annual rise in the cost of living, and then, rather than expanding their needs to meet their income, they expand their giving to invest the balance of their income for the glory of God. All income over and above the fixed ceiling can be given to the Lord. Another interesting idea is Ronald J. Sider's modest proposal for a graduated tithe. He says in an article in *Theology, News and Notes,*

> How about a graduated or sliding scale for our giving? We could sit down and carefully and honestly figure out what we would need to live for a year in reasonable comfort, but

without some of the luxuries . . . plus a certain amount for
each child. . . . We would give a tithe on the basic amount.
. . . Then, on the first $1000 over the basic amount, we
would give 15 percent to the Lord's work; on the next
$1000, we would give 20 percent.[2]

And so on. It's another very workable plan for people who
are serious about giving by God's standard.

3. *Method:* So, you've got your tithes and offerings in
your hot little hand. Or you have written the amount on the
check. Now, just to whom should you make that amount
payable? It would be simple, wouldn't it, if we could just
write "God" on the payable line and let Him take it from
there. But God uses earthly clearing houses. And the responsibility of stewardship comes into the picture again.
God does not rule out our intelligence or our responsibility
when it comes to giving. No merit exists in mindless,
purposeless giving of our tithes and offerings as we are
blown about by every breeze of fervent appeal.

We need to give systematically, prayerfully, and
thoughtfully if we are to be considered faithful stewards.
There are these three main areas to which our giving must
be directed under the leading of the Holy Spirit and the
teaching of the Word of God:

a. *Our local church.* Every local fellowship of believers
has material obligations which require its support. The
first concern is paying the pastor: "let the one who is
taught the word share all good things with him who
teaches" (Gal 6:6, NASB). The gaunt and starving preacher
should exist only among gaunt and starving people. God's
Word is clear about the responsibility of God's people to
attend carefully to the physical needs of the one who
labors for their spiritual benefit. A minister should live at
the average standard of living of his parishioners, neither
higher nor lower. If all tithes (as distinct from offerings)

were given to the local church, and half of them were used to support the general church budget, building maintenance, and programs, the other half of the tithes of every twenty families could support a minister at a wage representing an exact average of their incomes. It is something to think about, although simplistic, perhaps, in terms of large churches with huge buildings, many staff members, and multitudinous programs. Yet the principle remains: a lion's share of our giving, at least of our tithing, must be channeled into supporting our local church. As Pastor David T. Anderson, when ministering in Beulah Alliance Church in Edmonton, once put it: "You pay for your groceries at the store where you buy them—not at some other store down the street. So with your giving. You give your tithes where you and your family are getting the bread of life." If you find yourself unable to support the programs and ministries of the church you attend with your tithes, perhaps you should look for another fellowship whose message or method you can endorse more wholeheartedly, and to which you can give not only your time but also your tithe.

b. *Giving to further the proclamation of the Gospel.* This involves looking out beyond the local, community programs of your own church, and seeing the need for worldwide evangelism. It should be a priority item on every Christian's "gift list." If your church or denomination has a strong missionary program, you may direct your gifts through that channel. But I recommend that some of your offerings be saved for more personal giving. Many missionaries are proclaiming the Gospel of Jesus Christ while being supported solely by the monthly gifts of friends at home. And when you know such a "faith missionary" personally, or feel moved by the Spirit of God to support the work of one, you will experience that rare kind of joy I described early in this chapter: the joy of sharing in the work of that missionary or family.

To me the most important aspect of this kind of sharing is that it helps you to remember that missionary friend on a regular basis. Your giving has a face on it. And, as Jesus pointed out, "Where your treasure is, there will your heart be also" (Mt 6:21). The partnership which begins with giving matures into a prayer fellowship which means that you enter personally into the work of evangelism. Thus, even though your share of a missionary's support may be miniscule, that $5 or $10 a month (and don't promise support and then forget about it halfway through the missionary's term abroad) represents an investment of yourself in the missionary's work. Your family can join in the excitement of letters exchanged and furlough-time visits, and all of you will be enriched by this kind of fellowship.

*c. Physical needs of the hungry and suffering.* This is a third kind of need to which Christian giving must be directed. Giving to relieve the hungry, the destitute, the victims of catastrophe and others should not supplant our giving to the local church or to the cause of world evangelism. But in these days we should be giving more, over and above our tithes and regular offerings whenever possible, as we recognize our responsibility to relieve human suffering wherever we can. There are excellent Christ-centered and love-motivated organizations handling relief funds skillfully and with a minimum of waste. I believe that Christians should channel relief-giving through reputable, established, evangelical groups wherever possible, thus avoiding expensive bureaucratic inefficiencies in money handling which are commonplace to many secular aid organizations, and at the same time being sure that the gifts are given in the loving Spirit of Christ in which they are intended.

Day after day, as we flip the pages of our magazines and

turn on our television sets, we find ourselves looking into the eyes of hunger-haunted little ones, children of poverty, children of disease. And the ache becomes so great that we have to anesthetize ourselves. Or respond. Jesus' story of the sheep and goats in the great judgment day should be reread and restudied for its social implications today (Mt 25:31-46). We will, as nations, be judged for our generosity—or lack of it—to those in need. And if as nations, then surely as individuals we will have to give account for our responsiveness. Some of us will have much to give; some, very little. But all of us can give, remembering that God measures our giving not in terms of how much we give, but rather, in terms of how much we keep for ourselves.

Wesley, pondering the dilemma of the link between righteousness and riches, made a suggestion which is still valid today:

> Is there no way to prevent this continued decay of pure religion? We ought not to prevent people from being diligent and frugal; we must exhort all Christians to gain all they can and save all they can, that is, in effect, to grow rich. What way can we take that our money-making may not sink us to the nethermost hell? There is one way. . . . *If those who gain all they can and save all they can will also give all they can, then, the more they will grow in grace and the more treasure they will lay up in heaven.*"[3]

# 7

# BASIC NEEDS II: HAVING FOOD AND RAIMENT

## FOOD

One summer while I was in the hospital, I was fed intravenously for almost two weeks. As the technicians changed bottles and flicked the tubes to disperse bubbles, I thought about how much time I would save in my life if I just ate that way all the time. Just think, no time spent in food preparation or clean up. *Why, I found myself thinking, I could just sit at my typewriter all day every day, and eat through my hand!* Of course, the idea was ludicrous. For food is very much a part of our lives, and only when one is very sick does it seem as though another arrangement would be better. In personal spending, food often takes the largest single chunk out of our incomes, about 25 percent of disposable income being spent for it. And in daily living, food demands a good deal of our time and energy.

There's nothing wrong with that, of course. But it means that we need to be sure that we have healthy, sane attitudes toward food so that we can be good custodians of those food dollars, of that time, and ultimately, of our bodies. We should be aware that food is, first of all, for *nutrition*, and we must learn all we can about good, sound nutrition. Second, food is for *celebration*. Not just at special festive seasons, but daily as we gather as families, food is served for times of gladness, gratitude, and sharing. It seems a particularly perverse turn of events that our Western societies, which have access to the greatest amount of food, should have lost sight of the value of food both for nutrition (as food-habit surveys in both Canada and the United States show) and for celebration. Too many of our families eat haphazard meals, taken hastily and with little planning from a deep freeze or tin can, and plumped in front of television sets which prevent any kind of meaningful communication between persons, leaving each individual absorbed in his own world of vicarious experience.

When food is properly understood in its dual role of nutrition and for celebration, a family should meet at least twice a day—at breakfast and supper—around a table to partake of carefully planned if simple meals in an atmosphere of gratitude and love. Better in every way, for body, mind, and spirit, are simple meals lovingly prepared, gratefully received, and seasoned with the chitchat of a family about to disperse for the day or gathered together from the tasks of the day—than the most elaborate occasional ritual glutting of ourselves which has become the standard way of celebrating Christmas, Easter, and Thanksgiving, between which times meals are often eaten in a disorganized or tension-filled atmosphere. The writer of the Proverbs puts it poignantly: "Better is a dish of vegetables where love is, than a fattened ox and hatred with it" (Pr 15:17, NASB). I am not suggesting that festive foods should not be part of the celebration of special occasions. I am suggesting that, properly approached, every meal should be a celebration of God's goodness, of family love, of mutual interest and esteem.

Food, then, is first a matter of the head, as we study the basic facts of sound nutrition. And then it is a matter of the heart as we share it lovingly with our families and with others. Sharing a meal is still the most openhanded method of hospitality, the one which invites the outsider most deeply into the heart of your family life. Finally, food becomes a spiritual matter as we truly worship our Creator and Provider before each meal, not just in a mumbled grace, but in truly felt and clearly expressed gratitude. It is a spiritual matter, too, as we refuse to let our appetites become our god (see Phil 3:19).

With the permission of Canada's Food Prices Review Board, I am including here their very informative "Food Substitution List." The list shows ways in which the various food groups which each family should eat each day can be procured within various price ranges. Over time, choices could change because of relative price changes, but I think you will find the table helpful in planning for meals that will balance both budget and diet. On the reverse side of this table is a list of basic food groups based on the daily food guide known to—and ignored by— generations as "Canada's Food Rules." It is a simple, sane, and short guide. Perhaps you could clip out this one page and tack it inside a cupboard door where you can consult it frequently until your eating patterns conform to rules of sound nutrition and good-eating sense. I know that identical information is available to you through government-sponsored programs for improved nutrition, but here is a starting point from which you can work toward a thorough knowledge of nutrition. Two highly recommended books you may wish to proceed to are Edith Redman's *Recipes for Healthier Children* and *Recipes for a Healthier Family.*[1]

Probably the simplest rule, and perhaps the hardest to convert your family to if your eating habits have been casual, is the old rule of three "square" meals a day. A breakfast eaten together and including a cooked whole-grain cereal with brown sugar, milk, citrus fruit, or vitamin supplement (preferably "sanctified by the word of God and prayer," 1 Ti 4:5); a carry-along lunch with sandwiches containing a protein-rich filling such as cheese, sliced meat, or peanut butter, and a piece of fruit; a sit-down-together supper with meat, a cooked vegetable or two, and a green salad. These are the very simple building blocks of good nutrition. If your family likes to snack, be sure the snacks are nutritious. Stop having baked sweets, pop, or candy on hand. Let snacks be of sandwiches and fruit, and space them well before mealtime. Remembering that North America's number one nutritional problem is obesity, we should blush about our overeating habits.

## FOOD SUBSTITUTION LIST
### Choices Ranked on the Basis of Unit Cost of Key Nutrients

| First Choice (lowest cost per unit of nutrients indicated) | Second Choice (more expensive per unit of nutrients indicated) | Other Choice (most expensive per unit of nutrients indicated) |
| --- | --- | --- |
| **I. Milk and dairy products (calcium, protein and riboflavin)** | | |
| Skim milk powder | Cheddar cheese | Ice cream |
| | Cottage cheese | Ice milk |
| | Evaporated milk | Yoghurt |
| | Fluid milk | |
| | Process cheese | |

## II. Fruit (vitamin A and vitamin C)

Apple juice
  (vitaminized)
Cantaloupe (in season)
Grapefruit
Oranges (or juice)
Strawberries (in season)

Apples (applesauce)
Apricots
Bananas
Peaches
Pears
Prunes

Raisins

## III. Vegetables (vitamin A, vitamin C and folic acid)

Broccoli
Cabbage
Carrots
Mixed vegetables
Potatoes
Spinach
Squash
Tomato juice

Brussels sprouts
Corn
Celery
Green beans
Lettuce
Onions
Peas
Tomatoes
Turnips

Mushrooms

## IV. Bread and cereals (carbohydrates, protein, thiamin)

Bread—whole wheat
  (or enriched white)
Converted or
  brown rice
Flour (enriched)
Macaroni (enriched)
Rolled oats
Spaghetti (enriched)

Cereal (whole grain,
  flaked or shredded)
Cookies (oatmeal,
  peanut butter)

## V. Meat and alternates (iron and protein)

Baked beans
Eggs
Hamburger
Liver (pork or beef)
Peanut butter
Sardines

Bacon (back)
Beef (steak or roast—
  blade or chuck)
Beef tongue
Bologna
Chicken
Ocean Perch
Pork roast
Sausage
Stewing beef
Tuna
Turkey
Wieners

Bacon (side)
Cod
Halibut
Herring
Lamb
Salmon

Source: *What Price Nutrition*, Table 5 (Food Prices Review Board, 1975). Used by permission. Based on 1975 Canadian prices.

## BASIC FOOD GROUPS

Plan three meals each day and include selections from each of
the listed groups, according to the servings recommended.

Milk
Children (up to about 11 years)     2½ cups (20 fl. oz.)
Adolescents     4 cups (32 fl. oz.)
Adults     1½ cups (12 fl. oz.)
Expectant and nursing mothers     4 cups (32 fl. oz.)

Fruit
Two servings of fruit or juice. Include a source of vitamin C,
such as oranges and tomatoes.

Vegetables
One serving of potatoes.
Two servings of other vegetables. Include yellow or green and
raw vegetables.

Breads and Cereals
Bread, with butter or fortified margarine.
One serving of whole grain cereal.

Meat and Fish
One serving of meat, fish or poultry. Include liver occasionally. Eggs, cheese, dried beans, or peas may be substi-
tuted for meat.
At least three times a week, a serving of eggs or cheese should
be added.

Vitamin D
400 Internation Units of vitamin D should be supplied for all
growing persons and expectant and nursing mothers.

Source: *Food Rules*, Table 2 (Canadian Council on Nutrition, 1961). Used by
permission.

At least in the northern States and Canada, your family needs vitamin supplements on a regular basis. Ignore the suggestion that a balanced diet has all the vitamins you need. So many vitamins are lost in storage and cooking that I mightily disbelieve that myth. I disbelieve it on the basis of a long history of endlessly runny noses in our family, noses that suddenly dried up when I made vitamins a regular part of the meal scene. We take a multivitamin capsule which includes iron and an additional Vitamin C (100 milligrams) each day. And the result is resistance to infection, fewer days lost at school, and a generally healthy family.

Finally, learn to cook with leftovers. I wonder how we will answer to God for the good food that we have thrown out in our garbage while living in this hungry world! Even after Jesus had demonstrated His power to create plenty for the feeding of the 5,000, He commanded His disciples to pick up the scraps "that nothing be lost" (Jn 6:12). Leftovers are no insult; they are a challenge to creativity. Learn how to make—and enjoy—the poor man's staples: vegetable soups with a whiff of meat from a soup bone, slow-simmered stews, and shepherd's pie.

Along with developing sound eating habits, you will need to discipline yourself to sane shopping habits. A recent food-spending study in Canada showed that the average family of four spent $1,000 more per year than was necessary for sound and balanced nutrition. That's a lot of dollars, made up in small supermarket decisions that add up to unsatisfactory stewardship of the food dollars.

My good friend Sheryn had been teaching school until recently when she decided to stay home and care for her husband and a family of foster children. "I never thought of shopping as work before," she told me, "because I never even thought of looking at prices. I just bought what I wanted. But now, on a limited budget, shopping's really a tough job." She is learning to mentally compare unit prices, to look carefully for the best buys, and to put things back on the shelves because she has already overspent the amount she had allowed for that week. "After the last time I shopped," she said, "I had to go for a Coke to recuperate!"

Here are a few angles I have learned in the lean years that might help you keep the grocery cart a little lighter to wheel around:

1. *Shop from a list.* This will help you to avoid impulse buying, something which is promoted in every aisle of today's stores. Remember, your grocery store manager takes courses in how to tempt you to buy more than you need. You have to be prepared to outwit the most sophisticated psychological techniques as well as your own appetite if you are to keep your food basket uncluttered. Your shopping list can be made up in one of these two ways, both of which I have used:

*a. Draw up your list after planning your menus for the week.* This is a great idea for new homemakers, or for old ones who want to get out of food ruts. Planning this way will take you about an hour a week, after you have prepared a card index of menus with recipes to match. By following the basic food rules in setting up your menu cards, you can plan meals that are interesting and varied and nutritional. Then, looking up the recipes, you can list for purchase just those ingredients you will need for one week's meals. This is thrifty, and possibly the best way to teach yourself how to plan a balanced diet for your family.

*b. Keep a running list of basic food supplies.* This should be fastened inside a cupboard door or somewhere else handy, with every member of the family jotting down items which need to be replenished as they run low. While I used the method outlined above for the first few years of marriage, this is the method we now use for compiling our shopping lists. That's why my list may contain such items as "Toylet Payper." My seven-year-old makes her contribution to keeping up basic supplies.

2. *Shop only once a week.* This may not be practical if you walk to your store and carry home your groceries, although there are small push-or-pull carts (and I don't mean the ones that are supposed to be left at the store!) that you can get to carry home two or three bags. But if you drive to do your shopping, then once a week is the best way to shop. It has been my unfailing experience that every time I run into a grocery store for "some little thing" I neglected getting during my main shopping trip, I find myself picking up several other "little things," and food costs begin to escalate. Increasingly, the cost of transportation will force us to become even more efficient, perhaps making a major shopping foray only once or twice a month.

3. *Leave the children at home, or outside the store with their dad.* That may sound like female chauvinism, but one member of the family should become a food-buying specialist. Whichever one it is, he or she should do the shopping alone, or at least without the interrupting assistance of little children. My little ones can come with me only on the condition that they make no suggestions while I shop. Very autocratic, I know. But, "Could we have Munchios this week, please?" and "Mm—look at those cookies!" are just distractions to me. The older children (ten and eight) are occasionally enlisted to actually help me with the shopping, and I am teaching them how to shop—not just to buy. But the littler ones are usually left out of the store.

4. *Cut down on the number of canned and "almost ready" foods.* Most things are cheaper the further they are

from being ready for the table. And more nutritious, too. Peeling your own potatoes, baking your own brown beans, making your own soups, and buying macaroni or spaghetti cheaply in bulk instead of in ready-to-heat forms are just some of the ways you can trim costs. Make a minimum use of your can opener, even if it is electric, and you will serve your family foods with fewer additives. It makes garbage easier to handle, too.

5. *Skip the party foods aisle.* Tiny crackers, squeezable and disposable cheese containers with built-in waste that should make us writhe, and other tidbit foods are low in nutrition and high in cost. Use them only when you plan to have a party, but first consider less expensive alternatives, such as your own hot baked items. Your guests will be delighted with something plain and old-fashioned (one of the most memorable lunches I was ever served was homemade bread spread with butter and peach jam), and your budget won't take a week or two to rebound from its one-night stretching.

6. *Take it easy on the drinks.* Carbonated drinks, loaded with fizz and sugar and dye may be popular, but they are not a good nutritional investment. Save pop for special occasions. And avoid those powdered fruit drinks which have very little food value and some unadvertised risks to health in their highly colored and flavored powders. Buy real fruit juice and milk. Mixing whole milk and powdered skim in equal portions can lower the cost of milk for your family. If you are on a very tight budget, you can make savings by cutting out tea and coffee except for "company" occasions. At the considerable risk of sounding like a crackpot, I can assure you that hot water is cheaper, better for your health, and *can* be enjoyed!

7. *Ration your use of paper supplies.* Use old clothes to

make wipe-up rags that you can use, wash, and reuse instead of buying disposable wipe-up towels. Paper tissues can be stored in pockets for second or third uses instead of being tossed into the nearest wastebasket after one blow. (Of course, this thrifty system often means that they go through the washing machine, too!) When it comes to paper products, as with cans, what makes good economic sense makes good ecological sense, too. Just think, along with the dollars, of all the trees your family can save.

8. *Buy less sugar and few presweetened products.* The rise in sugar consumption, together with the rise in dental cavities, is a phenomenon of our recent affluence as a society. Your family can probably get along with very much less sugar than you currently use. Natural sugars contained in fresh fruits and vegetables are much better for you than processed sugar. And you can get used to meals without desserts, keeping the food expenditures down while keeping your weight down, too.

9. *Grow a garden.* It's a great project for the whole family, and the homegrown vegetables are a bonus in nutrition when picked and eaten fresh, or carefully canned or else prepared for the freezer. The savings on the vegetable aisle in the grocery store are noticeable, too.

Not long ago, I loaded an unusually large grocery order onto the cashier's turntable. Since Cam and I were going to be away for part of the week ahead, I wanted to make sure there were extras on hand for our temporary housekeeper. As Karen, the cashier, pressed the final total, she grimaced. "This is going to hurt," she warned.

"Oh, no!" I replied. "It doesn't hurt at all. I'm glad to have the kids to feed, glad to have the food to feed them, and glad to have the money to pay for it."

Karen broke into an open chuckle. "Now *that*," she

laughed, "is the nicest thing I have heard anybody say at this counter in a long, long time. You just made my day!"

It is in style to complain about the high cost of food. But perhaps it would be more constructive to look closely at our food-buying habits. The basic nutrients still can be bought at reasonable costs, and it is well to consider the fact that while "the average American family spends between 15 and 25 percent of its income on food, the average Indian family spends 80 percent."[2] Using our food money wisely will not only balance our own budgets but also encourage directions for the food industry which will place increasing emphasis on good nutrition at reasonable costs. Junk foods are manufactured because people buy them.

In this hungry world of ours, over one billion children live in developing countries where they suffer from hunger, disease, poverty, and lack of education.[3] We are fortunate to have only the kind of food problem we have: the problem of making wise choices. Instead of grumbling about the cost of food, we need to study nutrition and learn self-control. Let's "gird up the loins of . . . [our] minds" as Peter suggests (1 Pe 1:13) or tighten up our mental belts and, by using our heads, keep our bodies, and those of our families, fit temples for the Holy Spirit.

## CLOTHING

"Having food and raiment," Paul wrote to Timothy, "let us be therewith content" (1 Ti 6:8). Clothing is certainly one of our basic needs. In their book, *Figleafing Through History*,[4] Christie Harris and Moira Johnston attack the much-mouthed notion that clothing is basically either for ornamentation or seduction. Examining the history of costume, they conclude that clothing represents a very basic need of man: the need to be covered. From the Genesis account we know that this need has existed since the Fall

of man, all the streakers in the world to the contrary. And,
of course, our North American climate encourages a certain amount of modesty, if only for the sake of warmth.

Scripture gives us the reason for the basic need of clothing as well as the criteria of modesty and suitability (e.g., 1
Ti 2:9-10). Families who are trying to live the simple life,
either because they have reduced incomes or because they
have decided to share more, have to work it out from there.
These days, when what was once considered "poor
clothes" have become high style, we are freer than ever
before from the pressures to slavishly conform to the dic-
tates of haute couture. Clothing is freer, more individually
expressive, and more frank in its admission of economic
exigencies than ever before. The things that frugal people
have worn for years have worked their way upward into
clothing norms, and patches, once the embarrassment of
the lowly, are now the fad of the rich. All of this makes it
easier to dress a family on a limited budget. Here—from
our clothes closets to yours—are some of the things we
have learned about clothing ourselves and our family, not
only for "down on the farm" but also for the busy life of
politics, professions, and platform speaking, often on a
shoestring budget:

1. *Sewing and mending.* Torn and unmended clothes are
always unsightly, but a neat and creative patching job
combines simplicity with dignity. The wearer (or his
mother) is saying, "I care." Children from the age of nine or
ten can be taught to do basic mending such as sewing on
buttons or repairing seams. Once they can handle hand-
sewing jobs, they can be taught how to use the sewing
machine for machine mending such as patching. This
instruction should be for boys as well as girls. It's survival
training!

Every home needs a sewing machine, even if only for

mending. But it is worth remembering that home sewing is still the road to the greatest savings in clothing. By contributing labor, you can bring the price of a garment down from one-half to one-third the manufactured price. And you can make clothes with more generous seam allowance and more carefully reinforced seaming, all adding up to longer wear.

Careful fitting and meticulous pressing and finishing are the secret to make garments that look "handmade" rather than "homemade." I know numerous homemakers who earn pin money by extending their sewing skills to custom sewing for neighbors or drapery stores. So if you can sew, you can use your skills and your sewing machine to do double duty in stretching your family income.

I also know a woman who ministers with her sewing machine. To me. Elsie Jones is a dear friend of mine, a woman with daughters about my age, and an excellent seamstress. A fabric- and fashion-conscious person, she travels internationally at least once a year. And when I have some special occasion coming up, she is likely to say, "What shall we make you to wear?" Her contribution to my confidence in accepting speaking engagements across North America is immeasurable. It is the loving ministration of a special gift, and one for which I am most grateful.

2. *Recylcing.* There is no shame in wearing secondhand clothes, and now even the fashion magazines concur. Buying at "Thrift" or "Next-to-New" shops no longer has a social stigma. In fact, it is very "in" to wear a bargain. The whole trick, of course, is not to let it *look* like a bargain. The secret of smart and attractive dressing is not in expensive clothes, but in well-fitted and personally becoming clothes.

Hand-me-down packages have always been received like Christmas presents at our house. And any clothes that escape the ragbag by the time our four have worn them are passed on to someone else. Few of us have found ourselves doing the kinds of recycling we may well remember our mothers doing: taking apart old suits in order to make new ones; turning material over so that the worn side can be put inside. Today's new fabrics make sewing on older, dry-clean materials pointless. And yet, should we need to exercise such skills in order to keep our families warmly, modestly, and attractively clothed, these are things we could and would do.

3. *Shopping and selection.* Shopping for off-season specials is probably still the best way to buy new clothes at the lowest price. Winter clothing is expensive, but much less so if you can watch for the January clearings and outfit your family a year ahead. Recently a consumer program pointed out that department stores tend to work on a fixed mark-up margin, never really entering into price competition with other stores. Small shops, on the other hand, are often fiercely competitive, and so they may offer real price cuts at various times of the year.

Older children should have a right to a say in the selection of their clothing, but probably not the final word. Only an experienced mind can decide what is a "best buy," but parents should allow children to express preferences, or to choose between one or two alternatives selected by the parents. This helps children to enjoy their clothes more as they share in the responsibility of choice-making.

Nobody needs a lot of clothes. It is far better to have a few things that fit well and look great than a lot of clothes that just hang in the closet. One outfit for dress, two or three for school, and some "oldies but goodies" for work and play are sufficient for a child. Adult wardrobes need only to reflect the balance of time spent in various activities.

"Consider the lilies," Jesus said. From the field flowers,

we can learn not only of God's good provision, but the joy of individuality and variety, the fun of color and texture. Clothing, carefully chosen and tastefully worn, need not be an endless hassle and should not be a source of worry. Rather, as a carefully thought-through and well-planned part of life, clothing becomes a joyful affirmation of our personal dignity and worth, and a source of praise to God, the Giver of all good gifts.

# 8

# BASIC NEEDS III: A PLACE TO GO AND A WAY TO GET THERE

### Housing

Like many North American families, we are facing the complex problem of providing adequate housing for ourselves. While food and clothing are the "bare minimum basics" when it comes to needs, few would dispute that housing is an essential, too. Bewildered by ever-rising costs of home construction and struggling with straightening out real housing values (space for a family, sufficient individual privacy, warmth for our long, cold winters) from those confusing transferred values (status, snobbery, "pride of life"), we spend yet another winter in rented accommodations and think and pray and wait.

Part of the North American way of life until the last two decades has been not only a place to call home, but a place to call your own. Home ownership has been a major goal of young people as they establish themselves in marriage. Today the high costs of land and housing have pushed this possibility well out of the reach of many people, or pushed young married people into earning two incomes in order to meet staggering payments on large, long-term mortgage loans.

We have to face the fact that the inaccessibility of family homes reflects not only the high cost of housing—with increasing costs of material and labor—but also the cost of high housing. Today average people expect to live at a level which in previous generations belonged only to the rich. Television has piped the big dream into our living rooms for so many hours that we really begin to think of "home" in terms of the sets for television dramas. We have to struggle to remember that the shows have been brought to us, hour after hour, by the producers of consumer goods who want us to want things and who encourage us to develop extravagant tastes so that we will buy, buy, and go on buying.

I have learned a lot by living in the tiny house the Lord has provided for us as a "shelter in the time of storm." Our family of six lives in about 800 square feet of space (not counting a damp basement where there is a workbench and space for my washer and drier). There are three small bedrooms, two upstairs under the eaves. We have made the downstairs bedroom into an office, and Cam and I sleep in the living room on the couch which converts into a bed. As Geoffrey said the other day, "I guess you would really call this a multipurpose room. It's a family room, a living room, a reading room, a playroom, a music room, and a bedroom." But though we feel cramped, and certainly, compared with the houses of our peers, our housing is inadequate, we have to stop to remember that a generation ago, a family of four children lived and grew to adulthood in this very house. What has changed? Are children bigger now than they were a generation ago? Or are our housing concepts just bigger?

Actually, our big ideas of housing reflect our growing accumulation of things far more than they show a real need of vast space for people. It is particularly ironic to consider that as houses get bigger, families get smaller. Let's face it:

more and more people find they just cannot afford both the
big house and the big family! Because we have done a lot of
thinking about housing, we have observed some very re-
sourceful solutions to the problem of providing adequate
housing. Perhaps one of these will be the solution for us, or
for you:

1. *Work to save a down payment, and then buy a modest
house.* You can take a 25- or 30-year mortgage, recognizing that housing always *costs* (usually about 24 percent of
disposable income), but that real estate has customarily
responded to inflation. This means that your home, if well
maintained, is likely to increase in value over the years.
Home ownership has been one of the "small man's" surest
investments, supplying a basic need for his family as the
property value increases.

2. *Buy an older, run-down house in a less-than-
prestigeful district and have the joy of restoring it to life.* I
know a successful building contractor who started his
business in just this way. He moved into a tumbledown
house, fixed it up, built cabinets in it, and then resold it at a
handsome profit. Then he moved into another and did the
same, until he had his grubstake for launching a business.
You may find that this sort of inner-city housing is remarkably close to business and shopping centers, perhaps rul-
ing out the need for a vehicle, or at least for driving every
day. While factors such as the crime rate and the quality of
schools obviously have to be taken into account, there is
hope in this concept not only for lower-income families to
have simple homes of their own, but also for the renewal of
older communities as young people buy and restore such
properties. And it is a way of planting a Christian witness
in badly neglected areas.

3. *Buy a house with an apartment in the basement or
elsewhere.* Be sure before doing this to check zoning regu-

lations to ascertain that you can legally rent it out. Or move into a duplex and rent the other half. You will have to give up some of your privacy and some of the elegance of a place all to yourself, but the extra revenue could well cover your mortgage payments, thus making it possible for you to purchase your own real estate.

4. *Consider the possibility of building your own place.* This is something which more and more young people are doing now. You can buy precut houses, or save even more by buying the dimensional lumber and building a home yourself. Be realistic in estimating your savings, remembering that you will still have to hire subcontractors to do the work in which you are not skilled. And don't forget that it will take time and grit to see a project like this through to completion. Some additional precautions are: Be sure to check carefully the housing regulations covering the area where you intend to build; remember that you will need help and perhaps can work out a labor exchange with one or more friends. Outside of city limits (or even within some), you may be able to pour a basement and finish enough to live in it, and then build your house over your head.

5. *Build, or have built, a small house with a design and on a lot which are suitable to future expansion.* This may be a way to save interest if you can pay for the first part of the house before going on with the next phase. Cam's sister and brother-in-law, Barb and Ted Kent, have built a spacious family home in this way. Starting with a cozy two-bedroom bungalow when they were first married, they have expanded the house in two phases as the needs of their family have grown, imaginatively adapting a simple basic plan to meet their family's special tastes and requirements.

6. *If you already own a home, consider all the pos-sibilities for developing your present property.* Do this before joining the exodus to increasingly remote suburbs. A developed basement or attic or a built-on addition may be enough to make your house meet your family's needs, probably at far less expense than attempting to buy a new home at today's prices. When Barb and Jim Jones found that their three-bedroom bungalow, bought ten years ago, was beginning to feel a bit snug, they began to look at new housing. When they calculated the cost of a move to a larger house, they found that they could much more economically develop the one they already had. A base-ment development project, including the installation of a spiral staircase, a fireplace for their family room, and an additional bedroom and bathroom virtually doubled the amount of their living space at far less cost than the same number of square feet would cost at today's prices. My cousin, architect Roger Woods of Calgary, found a way to make a small old brick house big enough for his family through the ingenious use of the existing space and the planning (and hand-building) of an addition for kitchen and dining areas. There are many exciting ways to make your present home "do," providing you own it and can get city council approval for proposed renovations.

7. *A more radical idea, but one that is increasingly interesting to young families, is to solve your housing problems away from a major city.* Consider moving out to the country and buying an old farmhouse to rebuild, or building your own new home. But don't let the lure of the land draw you into an ill-advised move. Consider carefully the job opportunities suitable to your skills within a reasonable driving radius. A necessity for this way of life is dependable vehicles, probably two, since a wife left stranded ten miles from anywhere has a right to feel inse-

cure. So include the cost of extra transportation in your figuring. And be sure you get someone experienced in home building to estimate the cost of fixing up that romantic old house you fall in love with before you start in on something quite unrealistic.

The advantages of this approach to housing are becoming apparent to more and more young people who like the idea of raising their children away from the "thickening centre."[1] We are seeing farmhouses that have stood empty for years being bought and lived in. Five-acre plots can still be purchased in more remote rural areas for far less than an average city lot. I am not talking about moving to the plush acreage suburbs of a large city which are customarily inhabited by doctors, lawyers, and chiropractors. Rather, I am referring to getting far out into the country, a hundred miles or more from major cities. Only then is there any real economy in this concept. And I am not talking about "going farming" as a way to solve the housing dilemma. Farming is a big business and a risky one. Trying to live off the land is to reduce living to a subsistence, virtually no-cash level, which is very difficult for inexperienced or even experienced people. What I am talking about is practicing your trade or profession in a small town or city within a reasonable driving radius (probably 50 miles or so) and enjoying the quiet of country or small-town living. You can live for less in the country because you can grow your own garden, keep a cow, and raise chickens—and children—on a place of your own. You need fewer "good" clothes. But transportation is expensive and continuous. Utilities characteristically cost a great deal more than in the city. You have to develop and maintain your own water and sewage system outside of a town or city. So everything does not come up roses. But it is an option worth considering—carefully.

8. *Today's low-cost answer to housing is mobile or pre-built homes.* Mobile homes sometimes do not have the status, the eye appeal, or the prestige of other homes. And, unfortunately, many of the subdivisions in urban areas for mobile homes are unattractive and ridiculously crowded, becoming instant slums. However, more and more municipalities are beginning to zone proper-sized lots for mobile homes, recognizing that mobile homes do not represent transience as much as lower-cost housing, deserving of dignity as a practical solution to the pressing problem of housing for young families. One thing that must be weighed against the initial price advantage is that mobile homes have customarily depreciated in value, while properly maintained fixed dwellings customarily appreciate. Quality of insulation and of wiring needs to be carefully checked, since the fire hazard of mobile homes, with their large amount of flammable glue used in construction, must be taken into consideration.

9. *Obviously, apartment or semidetached dwellings will increasingly be the normal housing for most newly married urban couples and for many families as well.* Since there is a wide range of differences as well as costs in today's apartments and condominiums, this may be the kind of housing which you prefer, or it may be all that you can afford. Whatever the case, make your apartment home "a lamp shining in a dark place" (2 Pe 1:19, NASB), your family a Christian witness in the apartment or condominium complex in which you live. The very proximity to other people, which often affords many problems, can also offer limitless opportunities to befriend, to witness, to show the love and life of Christ. Many choose this type of housing, knowing that home ownership involves a multitude of other concerns and costs: lawns to be mowed, storm windows put up and taken down again, and an

endless round of maintenance. When I have watched apartment dwellers place their key cards in the automatic door opener of their underground parkade, I have mused about the simple life. All the folklore to the contrary, the simple life may well be apartment living.

Whatever the solution to meeting the housing needs of your family, remember that the real joys of any home are not in the size or shape of the physical plant, but in the spirit of love and contentment that prevails within the walls. Learn contentment in the situation in which you find yourself, and trust God to guide you in making necessary adjustments to make housing adequate for your needs.

### WHEELS

The ever-present cost pressure of owning and then of operating a family vehicle or two involves major decision-making. When friends of ours in the Los Angeles area, John and Karen Swan, decided they had to supplement their family station wagon with a second car, they found an old Ford with a lot of its gray paint chipped off. It was a kind of sad-looking outfit that their teen sons immediately dubbed "Dog Face." One of the boys' pals looked at the car and hooted, "What's that thing supposed to be?"

"That," said my friend Karen, with the immense dignity she saves for such moments, "is a one-payment car."

If you can afford to buy a new car and make the monthly payments, then skip the next little bit because it is for people who have to consider a secondhand car for one or both of their family vehicles.

"Buying a secondhand car is just buying someone else's troubles," the old saying goes. But no matter how you figure it, a secondhand car is cheaper than a new one. Look for a plain car: a four-door sedan, minus the luxury options. This kind of car has a low resale value, but you can probably buy it cheaply and "drive it into the ground." In addition, such a car was probably originally bought by low-speed, high-thrift people. Basic attractiveness is nice if you can find it, but simple dependability is much more important. "Will it get me there and back?" is my only concern with a vehicle. Good tire rubber is a high priority. I don't know about other wives, but changing tires is not my forte. I like to have a fair assurance that those wheels are going to keep rolling and that the tires are going to stay up. If you don't know a great deal about motors, get a mechanic friend to come along to listen to the engine and tell you what you might have to do to keep the car workable. Insist on seeing work orders for a tune-up or any other mechanical work that the salesman claims has been done recently on the car. And find out what kind of warranty the dealer offers. Thirty days is about all you can hope for—although some dealers give you ninety—but quite often all that is offered is half the cost of repairs. With a short warranty period, plan to buy your car at a time when you can give it quite a bit of driving in that time period to be sure that it is in reasonable running shape.

If your budget would allow for payments over a year or more, you can consider buying a better quality used car such as a demonstrator model. Car salesmen customarily drive the latest models and change to a new one when the next model comes out. Buying from a friend who has such a car is an unusually good idea. That lion's share first-year depreciation is off the price you pay; the mileage is likely to be low, and the treatment unusually meticulous.

Not every used car driven by a little old lady only on Sundays is in perfect shape. Buying a used car is always something of a gamble. Sometimes you end up with a lemon. But then, the same thing happens in buying new cars, and even the gilt-edged new car warranties have loopholes that leave buyers chewing their nails. In the years we have been married, we have driven both new and used cars. I see three equally sensible approaches to car purchase, any one of which may be just right for a family at a particular time:

1. *Buy a low-cost used automobile and drive it until it begins to be too expensive to keep in running order.* Then trade it or sell it and start again.

2. *Buy a used car of which you know the history, or one which you are sure is in good shape.* When Donna and Dennis Ross were a young couple expecting their second child, they bought a secondhand Buick, a lovely big car with all of the extras and 43,000 miles of use. Buying it in their small hometown, they knew the previous owner well and thus were able to be assured by him of the car's condition. Now, six years later and almost 100,000 miles further down the road and back, Donna and Dennis are still driving that car. Last summer, Dennis did a motor job. He's not a mechanic, but he worked under the supervision of a friend who was, doing the job during a long holiday weekend. Recently, a sparkling new paint job has made the old car look like new. Its original cost was modest. Apart from the motor job there have been only the normal wear-and-tear repairs: the universal joint, tires, brake linings. That old car still rides like a Buick, has all the automatic features of much newer cars, and looks great, too. These young people have been unusually shrewd about car economy.

3. *Buy a new car and drive it until it reaches the end of its tether.* Perhaps that will be eight or ten years, depending on the number of miles you drive per annum. This plan requires that you maintain the car carefully so that it outlasts all expectancies. The high depreciation of the first

year or two are spread out over as many as ten years, and thus a car bought new can be quite economical.

Of course, many people can afford to buy new cars every year or two. But others either cannot afford this car style or are wondering if there are not more useful ways of spending their money. More and more, people are availing themselves of short courses in mechanical know-how, borrowing or renting garage space, and doing minor and even major repairs on their own vehicles.

The scarcity of gas and its increasing cost are, of course, changing the family transportation scene noticeably. A major factor in any new- or used-car decision is gas-mileage economy. And we will be looking for ways to find our groceries—and probably our church fellowship—within walking distance of our homes, instead of trekking across our cities in endlessly crisscrossing patterns. Who knows? The cost of fuel may even have the effect of keeping families home together in the evenings, giving them a chance to get to know each other again. Many of us are learning to leave the car in the garage whenever we can, to keep lists so that we make a minimum number of trips to stores, and to walk or bike instead of driving. These "new" concepts of how to get around represent not only savings in expense but also improvement in general physical condition. Walking, jogging, and biking can give us the warm, happy, and slightly choking sensation that we are merely using up pollution instead of creating it.

A place to call home, a means by which to get away from and back to it again, plus our food and clothing constitute basic physical needs for which we can, in faith, claim God's supply, while at the same time being judicious in our choices.

# 9

# THE OTHER NEEDS

The young pastor's wife came home from the seminar, crushed and bewildered. "I guess I just don't have enough faith," she said.

"Enough faith for what?" I wondered aloud.

"Well," she explained, "the speaker was telling us how to budget our time and money. But she was so breezy about economic matters. She told us, 'I just believe God wants to give you all good things. Why, He just loves to give you the desires of your heart. Right now, I'm asking the Lord for a South Pacific cruise. And, you know, it's beginning to look as though one is shaping up for us.'" My friend came away sick at heart. "A lot of us just don't live on that plane. Is it lack of faith? The desire of my heart is to feed and clothe the kids on my husband's salary, never mind the South Pacific cruise!"

The young wife was quite right; most of us do not live on a plane where we have the liberty to desire some of the things which seem to come so naturally to many of the people who come to speak to us. For such a high standard of living to be held out as a norm, achievable by any who dare to exercise faith, is a travesty of Christian values.

A. W. Tozer writes scathingly, "So many professing Christians just want to get things from God. Anyone can

write a book now that will sell—just give it a title like
*Seventeen Ways to Get Things From God!* . . . Many people
seem to be interested in knowing God for what they can get
out of Him"[1] In another article, entitled "That Utilitarian
Christ," Tozer warns against viewing the Lord Jesus Christ
as "a kind of Aladdin's lamp to do minor miracles in behalf
of anyone who summons Him," and went on to say:

> The whole purpose of God in redemption is to make us holy
> and to restore us to the image of God. . . . He disengages us
> from earthly ambitions and draws us away from the cheap
> and unworthy prizes that worldly men set their hearts
> upon.[2]

From the Reformation acceptance of the intrinsic worth
of secular vocations, and the necessity for hard work
within those callings, we have moved so far toward complete secularization of our lives that we need to examine
carefully everything we read or hear to see if it sounds at all
like the lowly Jesus, the poor man who had no place to call
home, no coin with which to pay His taxes, no wealth
except that of the spirit. And before we lightly quote such
verses of Scripture as "No good thing will he withhold
from them that walk uprightly" (Ps 84:11) as magic pass-
keys to material blessings, we need to ask seriously
about God's purposes in our lives. We must always be
aware and afraid of treating God as some kind of heavenly
computer system which will spew out endless material
things for our enjoyment as long as the correctly pro-
grammed card is put in (the one with the notches punched
out over "faith" and "good living").

"God is a Spirit: and they that worship him must worship him in spirit and in truth" (Jn 4:24). He is concerned
about our material needs insofar as they constitute real
needs; Jesus taught us that in the Sermon on the Mount. If,
in His bounty, God should give us a measure of prosperity

over and above our needs, that is a gift of His disposing, not of our demanding. And it is given to us in trust.

A few years ago, some friends of ours listened to a sermon. The topic was faith, and the speaker told the story of two women, a mother and a daughter who were in need of winter coats. The mother prayed (as a member of the older generation might), "Dear Lord, I need a winter coat. Just anything, as long as it is warm, will do." The daughter (a true member of the modern society) prayed, "I need a winter coat, too, Lord. But, please, I would like it to be brand-new, size twelve, and green." Each woman got exactly what she had asked for, the preacher said. The gist of the sermon seemed to be: Ask for lots—the very best— and you will get it. Our friends took the sermon very seriously. They understood its message and acted on it. About to build a new house, they scrapped the modest budget-fitting plans they had been thinking about and built an extravaganza that has brought them to the brink of insolvency.

As economic pressures on the average family increase in the days ahead, we need to speak out against any kind of teaching that suggests that God exists to make us rich, that His special joy is in doling out things. Nothing could be farther from the spirit of the New Testament. There, the dangers of riches are solemnly warned against. There the norm is "Be content with such things as ye have" (Heb 13:5). There, earthly goods are something to be held in trust; a person's earnings are to enable him to care for his own family and to share with others.

I am sure that many of God's children have known times when God has been pleased to give them the sudden surprise of some delightful material gift. But for the one who is intent on knowing God, that thing, however wonderful it may be, is nothing compared with the hand that gives it, the hand of the great unchangeable Giver of all good gifts.

If we study carefully what Jesus said, we will understand that we have no need to be anxious about the supply
of our basic needs. They are our right as sons and heirs in
the family of God and will be supplied. But He gives no
warrant anywhere for whining and pleading with God for
more than our needs, and Paul in his emphasis on self-
control echoes His Lord. We can make our requests known.
That is our privilege. But to demand, to claim promises out
of context, and to expect that righteous behavior should
have some earthly tangible reward is to pathetically miss
the "high calling of God in Christ Jesus" (Phil 3:14).

Spurgeon, in commenting on the verse, "If ye shall ask
any thing in my name, I will do it" (Jn 14:14), makes this
thought-provoking observation:

> I may not ask for anything to which I cannot put Christ's
> hand and seal. I dare not use my Lord's name to a selfish or
> willful petition. I may only use my Lord's name to a prayer
> which He would Himself pray if He were in my case. It is a
> high privilege to be authorized to ask in the name of Jesus
> as if Jesus Himself asked; but our love to Him will never
> allow us to set that name where He would not have set it.[3]

I remember one spring when I had to wait for what
seemed an insufferably long time for my paycheck for a
part-time job I had taken. I had gone to the university
during the winter and had that familiar flat-broke feeling
many students have after eight months of steady with-
drawals and no deposits. Besides that, I had seen a suit—a
beautiful pink suit—in a downtown store. It was lovely
and well within the buying power of that check, if and
when it would come. Every time I was downtown I
looked to see if the suit was still there. And every time
the postman arrived, I looked for that check. Days passed.
Still no check. One day, fighting the disappointment of yet
another day without the paycheck, I was washing dishes in
our basement apartment and arguing with the Lord about

it all. "But, Lord, I've earned that check. Couldn't You lay it on someone's heart to get it out to me?" And the Lord spoke to me, so clearly that I set down the glass I was washing and listened. "You ask and do not receive, because you ask with wrong motives, so that you may spend it on your pleasures" (Ja 4:3, NASB). As I remember it, the Lord spoke in King James English, but the new translation may be even clearer.

I responded by simply giving up the pink suit. "OK, Lord, it's not a need. It's just a want. I'll forget it." When the check finally did arrive, I no longer wanted the pink suit at all. To me, far more wonderful than God's giving us every little whim, everything we want, is the complete and beautiful job He can do of taking a want out of my heart and then filling that little hole with joy and contentment.

Of course, over and above the basic needs, there are legitimate and recognizable needs of the human spirit, mind, and body. With some creative use of available resources, many of these can be met within limited budgets. And life can be full of "extras" without big price tags attached.

Richard, a hairdresser, chatted as he jerked my head and snipped my hair. "Some people I know, like, they seem to need to go to every training session on the continent. We had a girl, like, in one of our shops, like, who spent every holiday and all of her money traveling from one hairdressing course to another. I don't think it has too much to do with learning. Some people, like, just need to go to all those deals to sort of get pepped up—to believe in themselves. But me, I'd just as soon spend my holidays, like, relaxing. I can learn the new techniques from the trade magazines. Guys who run those short courses have gotten very, very rich because of people who just need that kind of inspiration."

I was interested in what that fellow said because it

can—with certain limitations—be applied to the endless conferences and seminars that many Christian people spend their time and money attending. We all need fellowship, we all need encouragement, we all need inspiration from time to time. And if we have the money to travel for these, that's fine. But if such programs are beyond the reach of our budgets, we need not despair. God is just as accessible from the square of linoleum that is my kitchen floor as He is from the loftiest mountaintop conference ground. And I am grateful for that knowledge and experience.

While many of my younger friends have knapsacked to L'Abri, Switzerland, and others of my age-mates have been able to travel halfway around the world to attend conferences, I have learned that the answer to the question, "Where could I go?" is simply "To the Lord." After our friends Ted and Isabel Quist came back from a trip to the Middle East where they attended a convention in Jerusalem, I asked Isabel what her dominant impression was. "Maxine," she told me, "I learned that I don't have to walk where Jesus walked to walk with Jesus." Amen.

I read catalogs of advanced learning programs in distant and exotic schools and colleges. And then I settle down to read in books what the best men and women in their fields have said and thought, and I grow mentally and spiritually right in my own home. I compile and read through bibliographies in areas of interest to me. I read and reread the Bible. I set myself a book for systematic study or I search the Scripture for light on a particular topic. And I go on growing—at minimal dollar cost. Someday I would like to engage in more formal study in any of a number of fields. But I do not have to sigh and resign myself to stagnation because such opportunities are out of reach just now.

The need of the human mind to know can be satisfied, if you have the means, by formal study or by travel. Lacking those means, it can still be satisfied—or better, whetted —by making use of library facilities. Travel to distant places may be beyond the family budget, but good books, maps, and a globe can help you visit faraway places at little or no expense from the warmth of your own home. Cultivating correspondence with various friends across the world will bring exotic foreign stamps to your mailbox while enlarging the world view of your whole family. Entertaining in your home those who can or must travel will bring the world into your living room.

We recall one evening when, in the little kitchen of our Alberta farm home, missionaries from Ethiopia met an agricultural exchange trainee from England. Our guests from Africa began to talk with our boarder from England, and within five minutes they discovered that they had a mutual acquaintance: a young woman who was a daughter of the missionaries' co-workers was in nurses' training with the fiancée of our exchange trainee. For a few exciting moments we felt like we were at the crossroads of the world!

Maintaining our oneness with the worldwide Body of Christ brings news from around the world into our home in the form of letters and mission magazines. We reach back out to that world in giving, in prayer, and in letters. Over the years, through Christian fellowship and other connections, we have established a network of personal friends so that now we have friends in almost every free country on the globe. When and if we should be enabled to travel, there will be friends to greet us wherever we go. That's one of the great pleasures of functioning as part of "the family of God." Meanwhile, with young children, we have found that the happiest vacations are those spent close to home. For our four children, frequent short jaunts to the lake twenty miles from our home, sometimes expanded into overnight camping, are probably more fun than would be the long and arduous trip to the nearest seashore.

There is a very real need of the human mind and spirit to perceive and to create things of aesthetic beauty. The God who "hath made every thing beautiful in his time" (Ec 3:11) is the one who, in making us in His image, has planted within us the desire for beauty. It is no pagan wish. Neither is it one which requires wealth to satisfy. Aesthetic appreciation can be developed even if your budget precludes you from concerts and performances of the fine arts. Television brings some fine performances into your home, at no greater cost than your time, and your patience in listening to the commercials. You can enjoy the best of good music on your record player, purchasing an endless number of listenings for about the price of a good seat in a concert hall. Museums and art galleries are customarily free to visit. And, again, there are books.

But, of course, aesthetic appreciation should not just be reserved for formal expressions. MaryLou Lepp, home on furlough from an appointment with Operation Mobilization, strolled with me down our lovely lane. "After the endless brown of dried-out northern Africa, the green is so beautiful," she commented. She noted the shades of green against the blue, late afternoon sky. "John and I have really come to appreciate the *ministry of nature*." Learning to see, to really see, the beauty of the world around us requires nothing more than the use of the senses with which we come equipped. And whether we look at the patch of sky that is ours from a city window or at a sweeping vista on a country road, we can feed our hearts on beauty until we simply burst into praise.

The desire to create things of beauty has been exploited in a booming business in craft kits and do-it-yourself (almost) outfits. Crafts and hobbies are an enrichment of life, but some of them may be out of reach when the budget is tight. Remember, though, that the essence of crafts is "creativity." Thus, the more creative you are in seeing the resources available to you, the more satisfying you will find them. You could try hobby-swapping with friends. When the excitement of their rock tumbler has passed, your family may have exhausted the possibilities of its candle-making equipment. So arrange an exchange. Again, the library is your pass to free and inexpensive crafts. Books abound to get you and your family started in developing an artistic or creative bent. If you cannot afford to oil paint, you can surely sketch with pencil or charcoal. And poetry has been written on all sorts of surfaces; you could even save the backs of envelopes for that!

Creative expression in music requires some sort of instrument (the least expensive, of course, is the voice), some training, and a great deal of persistent practice. I recently visited in a country home that was without running water or electric power. But an old upright Bell piano sat against one living room wall, with a propane lamp nearby and sheaves of music piled around. The lady, over eighty and bent with age, sat down and played pieces I would find difficult even to read. Her husband sang in a mellow—if somewhat quavery—tenor voice. He no longer plays his violin, he said, "But that grandson of mine, he can get a great tune out of that fiddle." Poor? Enriched by an afternoon of music with the Andrew Reimers, I thought not. Our little home is loud with music since the three older children all take piano lessons. We are blessed with such a lack of space that the piano and the television are in the same room. By the time three children have practiced after school, there is just no time for television viewing. Geoffrey and Cammie-Lou have each started on a second instrument now, and they delight in their own progress. Cam and I sit in the kitchen while in the living room Cammie-Lou picks out a tune on her guitar and in the study Geoff

blasts away on his trumpet. We want music to be part of the
intangible riches our children will come to value and to
share with others.

There is another need, both for mind and body, which is
hard for people on tight budgets to meet. Security. Over
and above a company pension plan, many try to make a
monthly deposit to a savings or guaranteed investment
plan of some kind. One of the cheapest ways to buy a
measure of economic security is through life insurance.
Perhaps the most important security is that both partners
have legal, properly made wills. "But we have so little,
what's the point of a will?" some have laughed. We were
shocked recently at a fellowship supper with six other
young couples, all with families, to find that three of the
couples had no wills. Even if just to name custodians for
your children, and to be sure that your survivor or children
do get what little may be in your estate, a will is absolutely
essential. It should be drawn in accordance with the laws
of your state or province, and updated annually. Don't put
it off!

In an age of spiraling inflation which means that even
savings plans or government bonds with relatively high
rates of interest represent a net loss in buying value of
dollars, trying to create relative financial security is very
difficult. Harold Lindsell writes in an article, "Advice to
Young Evangelicals,"

> I face an uncertain future. All that I have built to make
> retirement reasonably comfortable is being threatened.
> Every dollar paid into retirement benefits has suffered an
> erosion of purchasing power. If you are concerned about
> injustice, think of those who have been retired for twenty
> years and think of me in my retirement with a depreciated
> dollar. I am alarmed for my children and grandchildren
> who will be taxed so heavily to support my generation. It
> won't be pleasant.[4]

He speaks for a whole generation: people who faced the depression of the thirties early in their earning years and now face "the two polar horrors . . . : inflation and depression."[5] Families will need to pull together to assist their old; we, as members of the Church, will need to rediscover our responsibility to the needy among us. We are learning again, painfully, that security cannot be bought. Security can only be found in the fact that we do have a heavenly Father, in the knowledge that, having done the wisest thing we know how to do, we can rest on the promised provision of a caring God.

"Any valid inventory of human needs must include the therapy of leisure." So reads an advertisement of a large corporation, with the added note, "Our leisure living communities, pleasure cruises, travel trailers and motor homes are making life more enjoyable for many people." Ironically enough, the picture accompanying the ad shows a family out biking. Certainly recreation is a need, but it has been made expensive by our high tastes. It is time to remind ourselves that we can enjoy a lake without a boat. We can enjoy a boat without a motor. We can ski without driving to the mountains. We can enjoy the winter out-of-doors without a snowmobile. And we can even go camping without a trailer or a motor home. Honest. We have done these things. And so have many others like us.

Last summer, we took a short camping trip with our family, our total gear being our ten-year-old nine by twelve-foot tent, a Coleman cookstove, and sleeping bags. At Park Lake near Lethbridge we found a fairly quiet nook in which to pitch our tent, and then strolled down to the pleasant, shallow lake for an evening swim. As we walked back, we found that we were going to have an opportunity to observe a contrasting camp style at very close range. Squeezed into the site next to ours was an enormous motor home.

Our first greeting from the new arrivals was a marshmallow, under done or over done, tossed onto the road. We just managed to miss squishing it between our bare toes before composing our faces for a neighborly "Hello." We found the new neighbors friendly. Very. Perhaps their children had never been in something so quaint as a tent before, because they explored it thoroughly. *It's always fun to see how the natives live,* I thought to myself.

The marshmallow roast was still going on. "Want a marshmallow, little kid?" their children asked one of ours. Our children had never seen such big puffy marshmallows. Ours were the smaller, staler, two packages-for-a-dollar variety. When our children offered to bring their own marshmallows and toast them at the fire, the others just laughed. "What do we need your marshmallows for, kid? We've got lots." The parents sat and chatted at the picnic table while Cam and I tried to do a bit of camp cooking. Were we going to fry our steaks in that little cooking pot? "Martha, go get our big skillet for these people." Was it getting a bit too dark for me to read? "Martha, get that big flashlight."

The party broke up early. "We've got to get an early start," the father explained. "We're going to do the mountains tomorrow." I thought about that as I crawled into our little tent. Do the mountains tomorrow! Alberta's Rockies? Should make a fairly full day! Except for the insistent barking of our neighbors' huge German shepherd, the quiet night beside the lake was undisturbed. Then, soon after six in the morning, the sound of a mighty motor filled the somnolent campground. The great engine fired, roared, then died. Again. And again. Inside our tent, the smell of raw gas was choking, and I was bidding a tearless "Adieu" each time the motor fired hopefully. Finally, the motor took hold, and after several long, throaty revs, our neighbors roared off. They were having a wonderful camping trip, they had told us.

But more and more, young families are seeking their leisure and recreation in activities which are quiet, use muscles instead of motors, and—where possible—can be done "far from the madding crowd." The beauty of it all is that many of these activities can be enjoyed at minimum cost. There never has been a price put on a sunset. Or moonrise. Or the quiet glow of a dying campfire beside a quiet lake. Or the high-pitched hum of that one last mosquito you failed to get out of the tent at zip-up time.

Our spiritual need of food and fellowship, our intellectual need to know and grow, our creative need to make and enjoy beautiful things, and our psychological need for security and "unwinding" through recreation are all needs known to our heavenly Father. He is aware of our needs, as we should also be. Whatever our standard of living, He can help us to creatively design patterns by which we can meet these needs for ourselves and our families. In this light, we can say with assurance:

> The LORD God is a sun and shield: The LORD will give grace and glory: no good thing will he withhold from them that walk uprightly (Ps 84:11).

# 10

# PUTTING THINGS IN THEIR PLACE

It was just before Christmas. Cam and I were finishing up a bit of shopping at a large city mall. We had done a lot more looking than buying, I in my much-worn leather jacket, Cam in his jeans, with very little money in the pockets of either. As we stepped outside, I noticed an elegant woman drive up to the parcel delivery depot in a big white Lincoln. Her strawberry-blonde hair was beautifully swirled, her makeup meticulous. I couldn't help but smile to myself at the obvious contrast between her economic condition and mine.

Then, as the young woman, wrapped in a luxurious fur, stepped out of the car to give directions to the boy carrying out her parcels, our eyes met, and we gasped with the shock of instant recognition.

"Peggy!"

"Maxine!"

She was a high school girl friend with whom I had long since lost contact. We stood together on the sidewalk, chatting eagerly about the years that had intervened between high school and this moment. Peggy had done secretarial work in several large cities; then she had married a lawyer. "I'm so glad things have gone so well for you, Peggy," I told her.

"And how about you?" she asked. The physical realities of our situation were, at that moment, almost painfully apparent. "Well," I said, "we're trying to get started in farming, and our youngest child is just nine months old."

"Your youngest?" Peggy asked. "You have how many?"

"Four," I said. "Two girls and two boys. They're beautiful."

A shadow went across her eyes. "You lucky thing," she said. "We still don't have any. But we're hoping."

As she slipped back into her big, beautiful car, Cam and I waved good-bye and walked across the parking lot to our current secondhand Chevrolet wondering which of two classmates was really the richer.

A friend of ours who also lost very heavily in the cattle business reversal that dumped us overboard, told us, "My men keep asking me why I'm smiling. And I just have to tell them that if I'm healthy in body and relatively stable in mind—and if on top of that I have life in my spirit through faith in the Lord Jesus Christ—then, man! No matter how much money I may have lost, I am still a wealthy man!"

What is poverty? What is wealth? No field could possibly be more relative than this. Today, of course, we are helped in our definition of poverty by the annual statement of government offices concerning the "poverty line." Radio announcers and newspaper writers grab up the releases from our economic councils. We read it; we hear it. "Any family of 3.7 with a net earning of less than $XY,000 per annum is living—officially—below the poverty line."

We did not know about the poverty line when we were kids. Looking back to our childhood, my brother once exclaimed, "We were poor, but we never knew it." Poor we may have been; poverty-stricken we were not. We had all the best of everything that really mattered. With good and godly parents, lovingly providing for far more than our physical needs while building a modest family home quite literally over our heads with their own hands, we children were anything but poor. Our personalities were sustained by love and encouragement; our minds stimulated by exposure to ideas, books, and interesting people; our spirits nurtured on the truths of God's Word, daily read and taught, and—more important—lived before us. When I go back to the city of Lethbridge and drive nostalgically down Twelfth Avenue South past the house where my most precious "little girl" memories took place, I am always surprised to see how small the house and yard are. By today's standards, our home was tiny. But to four growing children, it was home. We lived in the basement while our parents built the upstairs. And when the upstairs was completed and we "moved up," what joy! Our living area was doubled overnight. And we were the "kings of infinite space."[1]

Today, it is much harder for families to keep the simple joy of not *feeling* poor, since government pronouncements and figures create "a climate of psychological poverty . . . that has little to do with what is really going on."[2] Having conducted a poll concerning attitudes toward poverty and riches, Martin Goldfarb concluded: "Poverty . . . is more than a physical thing, it's more than being deprived of dollars; it is an attitude, a sense of defeat, a loss of dignity."[3] For this very reason, government enunciations of the "poverty line" are misleading at best and, at worst, severely damaging. It is one thing to be poor. It is quite another to be told you are poor.

It is hard to work out a clear idea of relative poverty and relative wealth. Between the government telling us at what income we are poor or underprivileged, and the television presenting dramas on palatial show-home sets, it is hard to get a balanced idea of what real poverty or real wealth consists. Perhaps we have to turn to history, to read of the discomforts experienced by even the wealthy of two or three centuries ago, in order to understand the wealth we have in what we consider to be just ordinary, accepted comforts. Perhaps we have to come to terms with the housing conditions of the average peasant of the Middle Ages. Or really get an understanding of how the *average* person in many areas of our world lives today. Perhaps we need to go without a meal or two to find out what hunger really feels like. There are standards by which all of us, even the most pressed, are actually wealthy. There is a sense in which feeling "poor" or "rich" depends only upon to whose condition you compare your own.

There is, of course, such a thing as poverty. Real poverty. It is a miserable state of grinding necessity. When there is unremitting pressure in trying to make an income go around necessities—food, clothing, housing, and transportation—then there is, indeed, poverty. And poverty has its negative effect. It distorts the value of money. "More money" becomes very important. A person begins to dream of windfalls. And materialism becomes just as real a problem to the family which is truly experiencing poverty as it is to the very rich who also might be dominated by thoughts of material things. Or more so.

But physical, lack-of-money poverty is really only one aspect of the kind of impoverishment which cripples the human spirit and hampers the total growth of the individual. We need to develop discernment in a number of areas if we are ever to be released to enjoy the riches we may already have and are not recognizing as such.

First, to understand what state constitutes wealth and what constitutes poverty, we must distinguish between the temporal and the eternal. It is important for us as Christians to understand and live in the light of the fact that the *real* world is the eternal one. The things of this life, no matter how good or how many, are only trappings of a

temporary earthly existence. Therefore, real riches must be
spiritual riches, things which will outlast this earthly existence. This is what Jesus taught. This is what Paul reiterated: "If ye then be risen with Christ, seek those things
which are above, where Christ sitteth on the right hand of
God. Set your affection on things above, not on things on
the earth" (Col 3:1-2).

We need to remember that because the physical is so
immediate to us—as pressing as our own skins—and because it is proclaimed as the real world by so many forces
which press physical and material needs and wants upon
us, even as believers in a resurrected Christ, One who has
pioneered the way into the real, eternal world for us (see
Heb 6:19-20), we may forget where our real interests lie.

Writing instructions to a junior devil on how to tempt a
new Christian away from discipleship to Christ, "Screwtape" says:

> The sense of ownership in general is always to be encour-
> aged. The humans are always putting up claims to owner-
> ship which sound equally funny in Heaven and in Hell and
> we must keep them doing so. . . . We produce this sense of
> ownership not only by pride but by confusion. We teach
> them not to notice the different sense of the possessive
> pronoun—the finely graded differences that run from "my
> boots" . . . to "my God."[4]

In a well-known essay on "The Blessedness of Possessing
Nothing," Tozer describes the craving to possess as "a
tough, fibrous root of fallen life whose nature is to possess,
always to possess." He says:

> The way to deeper knowledge of God is through the lonely
> valley of soul poverty and abnegation of all things. The
> blessed ones who possess the Kingdom are they who have
> repudiated every external thing and have rooted from their

hearts all sense of possessing. . . . These blessed poor are no longer slaves to the tyranny of things.[5]

Let's face it: real poverty is the lot of every one of us—from those who work hard at wrapping inadequate incomes around the needs of a family to those who have so much that they are bored—if and when material things are first, and when this temporal world is treated as most important. Real poverty is the burning desire to possess, to claim more and more things as "mine." From this need to possess stems all sorts of contentions (see Ja 4:2-3). From this need to possess comes the continuous and much-encouraged breaking of the tenth commandment: "Thou shalt not covet" (Ex 20:17). From this need to possess comes our unending greed and insatiable sense of need.

The richest people in the world are those who are aware of the spiritual, eternal dimension of life into which we enter by faith. These people know that the real things are the things that cannot be seen with the eye.

Another distinction we need to learn to make is between those things we need for physical survival in this temporal world and those things we merely crave in order to boost sagging egos, to confirm our identities somehow, or to project a success image. Joy Duncan, a writer friend of mine, commented in a letter to me:

> People . . . suffer these days from a lack of identity. So many are caught in unrewarding jobs without the struggle and sense of direction our pioneers had simply to stay alive. It's a willy-nilly kind of existence. So they compensate by striving for things—"I know who I am now. I'm the owner of a new car." "Look at me. I'm somebody because the neighbors come to swim in my pool." It's a basic lack of self-worth that is alleviated by comparing oneself, favorably, with others—and, of course, if you can't compete in the "things" sweepstakes or don't measure up, it is devastating. It would be so simple if people would believe in

themselves—which, as you point out, is a spiritual thing. If
we are important to God, what else can matter?

We need, too, to distinguish between real faith in God
and a mere faith in things. Turning Christianity into a
"faith in God for things" is a sad, materialistic travesty of
the Gospel which has rooted itself stubbornly in our consciousness. Jesus told the story of the rich man whose life
consisted merely in getting more and more, a man whose
epitaph throughout the ages has been "Thou fool" (Lk
12:20). And while we remember well the story, we often
forget its pointed application: "So is he that layeth up
treasure for himself, and is not rich toward God" (12:21).
We begin to experience real riches when we stop looking
to God as a supplier of things, and begin to seek Him for
Himself. Two stanzas of A. B. Simpson's hymn, "Himself,"
tell the story of one who learned to live a life "rich toward
God."

> Once it was the blessing, Now it is the Lord;
> Once it was the feeling, Now it is His Word;
> Once His gift I wanted, Now, the Giver own;
> Once I sought for healing, Now Himself alone. . . .
>
> Once it was my working, His it hence shall be;
> Once I tried to use Him, Now He uses me;
> Once the Power I wanted, Now the Mighty One;
> Once for self I labored, Now for Him alone.[6]

Another hymn expresses a similar experience succinctly:

> My goal is God Himself, not joy, nor peace,
> Nor even blessing, but Himself, my God.[7]

It is only when I can truly say that my life goals are bound
up in knowing and growing in God that I can dissociate
myself from lesser, material goals and direct my energies
in prayer and in life toward bringing pleasure to the heart

of the One "who loved me, and gave himself for me" (Gal 2:20).

Real poverty must be ultimately described in spiritual terms. It is "having no hope, and without God in the world" (Eph 2:12), the condition of those who do not know Jesus Christ as Lord and Saviour. It was this kind of poverty that Jesus came to eradicate. Certainly He was concerned about physical needs. He fed the hungry. He healed the sick. And all without charge. He lived the simple life and shared all that He had and was with others. But over and over again He pointed out that the deep need of the soul could never be satisfied with bread alone. It is as we recognize the inner emptiness of our spirits and come to Him that He meets our deepest needs. He fills our hungers with Himself, the living bread. He satisfies our thirst with Himself, the living water. He supplants our cravings for "things" with Himself.

Real poverty is to be without Christ. Or, having made a profession of salvation, not to find our very beings saturated and blessed by His presence. Real poverty is to want things—anything—more than we want God. Real poverty is to have our lives cluttered, the good seed of God's Word "choked with cares and riches and pleasures of this life" and thus bringing "no fruit to perfection" (Lk 8:14).

Ultimately, we can conclude that real poverty is that state of mind when things are uppermost. Real poverty is when hunger pangs force from my mind all thoughts but those of food. Real poverty is when the children are not dressed warmly enough for winter. Real poverty is when the housing we can afford is not adequate to the needs of our families. On the other hand, real poverty is— equally—when I have eaten so much that I am uncomfortable, and again, my thoughts center on food. Or when I have so many clothes that I have to spend a lot of mental energy making choices among them or finding ways to

store them. Or when, regardless of my living conditions, I
am discontent and brooding about how to have more. Real
poverty is when material things are most real and most
pressing in a person's mind. It is poverty—and, indeed,
slavery—because the human mind and spirit are made for
higher things, higher pursuits. When the mind becomes
trammeled, either through need or through overabun-
dance, by mere things, it is rendered useless for more
meaningful pursuits. A girl in a group I once led, Barbara
Midgley, wrote this little Haiku:

> Like a bird, I soar
> Heavenward, My spirit free—
> Then earth pulls me down.

When earth pulls us down, we are poor.

There is, however, a kind of poverty that Jesus called
"blessed." He did not consider it blessed to be cold or
hungry or homeless. But He called it blessed to be "poor in
spirit" (Mt 5:3). Actually, we are all poor in spirit. Spiritual
poverty is our legacy from spiritually bankrupt Adam (see
Ro 3). But Jesus calls us "happy" or "blessed" when we
recognize our poverty of spirit and turn to God in repent-
ance.

In the book of Revelation, letters addressed to two different churches give us insight into the real meaning of
poverty and riches, not from our own, natural point of
view, but from God's. To the church in Smyrna, the Spirit
directed this message: "I know thy works, and tribulation,
and poverty, (but thou art rich)" (Rev 2:9). Here, a church
which was suffering deep physical poverty was warmly
reminded of its spiritual inheritance. "Blessed are the poor
in spirit," the letter echoes, "for theirs is the kingdom of
heaven" (Mt 5:3).

The Spirit directed quite another kind of message to the
church of Laodicea:

> Because thou sayest, I am rich, and increased with goods, and have need of nothing; and knowest not that thou art wretched, and miserable, and poor, and blind, and naked: I counsel thee to buy of me gold tried in the fire, that thou mayest be rich; and white raiment, that thou mayest be clothed, . . . and anoint thine eyes with eyesalve, that thou mayest see. As many as I love, I rebuke and chasten: be zealous therefore, and repent (Rev 3:17-19).

To be spiritually bankrupt and physically rich was the great problem of that church, and the tragedy of many of us today. There is no blessedness in that kind of poverty. But to be poor in spirit and to know it—to recognize that all of our adequacy is from God—that is the happy state described by Jesus as leading to possession of the Kingdom of heaven.

Paul wrote a strong pass-along warning to young pastor Timothy, advising him against "men of corrupt minds . . . supposing that gain is godliness" (1 Ti 6:5). For Timothy, Paul put the Christian philosophy concerning material things into a nutshell: "Godliness with contentment is great gain" (1 Ti 6:6). If we could just get ahold of that statement, writing it over our doorways, however humble or lofty they may be. Great gain, real profit lies in (1) godliness, and (2) contentment.

What is godliness?

It is simply God-likeness.

It consists, first of all, in having spiritual life. We are born spiritually bankrupt, spiritually dead (Eph 2:1). And only as we receive the vitality of the living Lord Jesus Christ into our lives by faith can we experience what Jesus called the "new birth" (see Jn 3:1-18). Godliness begins with spiritual birth. But it does not stop there.

Godliness is seeing things as God does: the things of this world as good in that they add comfort to our short stay on this earth, but as secondary in importance to the real things which are spiritual and eternal. The things of this world as loaned only as a trust for which we will be called to give account. Godliness is using the good things of this life as God would, as a means of bringing blessing to others. Paul outlined three reasons for diligence in business:

1. to be able to pay our debts and live honestly (Eph 4:28; 1 Th 4:11-12);

2. to provide for ourselves and our own families (1 Th 4:11-12; 1 Ti 5:8);

3. to share with those who are less fortunate (Eph 4:28).

We can only develop godliness, or a godly perspective on things, as we deepen our devotional life, as we read the Word of God daily and soak up its revelation both of ourselves and of our God. And we will always be challenged in our quest for godliness by that standard set by our Lord Jesus Himself: "Be ye therefore perfect even as your Father which is in heaven is perfect" (Mt 5:48).

If we really claim to be children of God through faith in Jesus Christ, then the first quest of our lives must be godliness. That's what Jesus was talking about when He said, "But seek ye first the kingdom of God, and his righteousness," with the promise that all our temporal needs would be met on that condition (Mt 6:33).

Whenever "things" become central in our lives, whether those things are legitimate enough in themselves or not, then—if we are truly children of God—we can expect that His Holy Spirit will bring pressures to bear to move those things out of the center of our hearts and thoughts, out to the periphery where they belong. For the center of our beings must belong to God alone.

And then, going back to Paul's phrase describing "great gain," godliness is to be with contentment.

Contentment is the key to the restful, rejoicing Christian life. Godliness first. And then, with God at the center of our lives, contentment follows. Things become only as important as they should be: necessary to sustain physical life, but not necessary to build up our egos or to maintain a special status. As we mature in our walk with our Lord, things should lose their luster and their appeal. Certainly, the more time we spend looking into the face of Jesus in devotional worship, the less interest the things of this world will hold for us.

In a recent phone call, my friend Donna told me, "Oh, Jerry thought about taking an extra job this winter, when the farming's a bit slack, so that we could finish up our basement. But I talked him out of it. You know, a few years ago that would have seemed mighty important to me. But now I know that the time we spend together as a family is far more important than wallboard on the rumpus room. It's funny how you get weaned from things, isn't it?"

I knew exactly what she meant. Two or three years ago, when we thought we might be able to build a house, the idea consumed me. I spent hours making sketches, studying plans, scanning home magazines. And the Lord removed the possibility of building at that time. Now, with house plans again on the kitchen table, I find that I am interested only in making good and wise choices. The house has ceased to be a thing of importance in itself; it is now just a means to the end of fulfilling our responsibilities to our growing children and of being settled so that we can serve the Lord effectively in the ministries He has entrusted to us.

When we know the basic provision of day-by-day needs, claiming by faith our daily bread; when we have healthy and secure children; and when we experience love and joy in our relationships with others, both within and outside of the home, then we are really rich. And when we can know God as our Father through faith in Christ, and live in fellowship with the whole Trinity, then our wealth is beyond all reckoning.

The good life, as I see it, is the uncluttered life, the life in which the main goals are spiritual, the life in which the main riches are eternal. If along the way God should entrust to our care physical goods as well, then that is a responsibility just as much as a privilege. We need to be prodded into remembering that real security can never be found "in uncertain riches, but in the living God, who giveth us richly all things to enjoy" (1 Ti 6:17).

Real poverty is to fail to discern where the real world lies.

Real wealth is to recognize the spiritual world as the real one.

Real poverty is to depend on things for identity or status.

Real wealth is to find our true worth in the love of Jesus Christ.

Real poverty is to depend on things for security or for happiness.

Real wealth is to come to God for these things which only fellowship with Him can bring into our lives.

Real poverty is to be thing-dominated in our daily lives.

Real wealth is to have our lives centered on the Lord Jesus Christ.

The good life is not one which can be defined as being above any arbitrary poverty line. It is, simply, "godliness with contentment." It is simplicity with dignity. It is having without holding. And that is—not only now, but eternally—"great gain."

# 11

## WHERE WE'RE AT

Not many months ago, I sat in the shade of the historical reconstruction of fur-trading Fort Edmonton and chatted with historian Dr. J. G. MacGregor about conditions, past and present. A regional writer, he has himself lived through enormous changes here in western Canada. He spent his first winter in Canada in a tent, something which those of us who survive our bitter winters in warm houses find almost unimaginable. "Things will change back," he said. "It is inevitable. I don't think they will get as hard as they were for the early pioneers. But nowadays a young woman thinks nothing of going downtown and buying a new dress every other week. In the old days, it was an event to get new clothing once a year. And it will go back to that. I would say in as few as ten years, the economy will be slowed down to that extent. And let's face it," he added thoughtfully, "it won't be all for the bad."

Those of us who read our Bibles and are aware of biblical prophecy know that Dr. MacGregor is no doubt right. Widespread economic chaos and famine are predicted in the book of Revelation. Both are now upon our world. But surely this is not a time for Christians to go about with worried frowns, clutching frantically at our diminishing consumer power.

The call to reconsideration of our life-style is being pressed upon us by a number of economic facts: recessions, inflation, the clamorous needs of the third world. It is a call which is being issued by politicians as well as preachers. The Canadian Prime Minister recently called on the Canadian people, "not for sacrifice, but for restraint." But it was our Lord Himself who issued a far wider call almost two centuries ago:

> Do not lay up for yourselves treasures upon earth, where moth and rust destroy, and where thieves break in and steal. But lay up for yourselves treasures in heaven, . . . for where your treasure is, there will your heart be also. . . . You cannot serve God and riches (Mt 6:19-24, NASB marg.).

A few years ago the call for restraint was neither so pressing nor quite so inescapable. For the Christian young person growing up when I did, there seemed to be two main vocations or callings. One was to "full-time service," which meant limited income, but presumably adequate rewards in nonmaterial terms. The other equally honorable calling was to enter a career of your choice and, with any luck at all, to get rich. Not necessarily really wealthy, mind you. But by any global standard comparison, rich. The Christian press was turning out a spate of "success stories" for an eager, but not always perceptive, audience which gradually came to equate riches with righteousness, and financial acumen with faith. The super-successful businessman or professional person was promoted as the image of the *average*, or at least the *normal* Christian.

It all added up to a prevailing feeling that anyone who didn't "make it," on the same standard of success which the world around us used, was somehow a second-class citizen not only in society as a whole, but in the Church of Jesus Christ as well. The "gold ring principle," whereby the "man . . . in goodly apparel" had obvious preferment

within the Church (see Ja 2:1-10), became an obvious fea-
ture of even our evangelical churches.

Of course, this development can be given a broader
historical setting, and by doing so we can help ourselves
understand the assumptions on which we have built our
value structures, structures which now, in the white light
of the "present distress" seem to be so inadequate and so
unscriptural.

First of all, there is the immediate historical context. Our
parents' generation lived through the Great Depression.
The "dirty thirties" left an imprint on the mind of every
person who passed through them, an ineradicable memory
of pressing poverty which created a desire for things: not
just for things in themselves, but for things as an indica-
tion of security. As with food-deprived rats in psychological experimentation, the hoarding instinct of people who
knew the deprivation of the thirties had deep inner roots.
People who lived through those days wanted to be sure
that they themselves would never know that kind of pressure again, and to be certain that their children would not
have to go through such an experience of poverty. Making
money, saving money, and buying things assumed an importance out of all proportion to need in the shadow of the
great want of the 1930s.

The same phenomenon has been seen in immigrants
who came to North America in the wake of the European
holocaust of World War II. In high school days, I had a girl
friend who with her parents had lived in refugee camps
after the war. She still spoke with a heavy accent, and even
then her eyes had the haunted look of a child who had
known hunger and cold and fear. I found her family, a
Christian family, astonishing in its continuous talk and
thought of "things." The accumulation of things seemed
to obsess every waking hour for every family member.
And, of course, with thrift and hard work, they were catch-

ing up quickly with their neighbors in material possessions. Such aggressive acquisitiveness cannot be
criticized without a sympathetic understanding of its
psychological basis.

A second fairly immediate historical aspect of our acceptance of wealth as a worthy goal in life lies in the
history of the evangelical movement itself. This movement, and especially that part of it which in North America
has been known as "fundamentalism," has been a movement of the poor and of the uneducated. And, as is well
known in sociological studies, when any semi-outcast
group begins to become socially acceptable, a very strong
emphasis is placed on those things which bring upward
mobility and respectability: education and wealth. Thus,
in our conservative evangelical circles, we have in recent
years tended to exalt those persons who are better edu-
cated and those who are more wealthy as the leaders who
can bring us acceptance in our larger society.

These historical and sociological factors help us understand how the "company of the redeemed," named for a
man who had "not where to lay His head" (Mt 8:20), has
become a "company of the rich," or at least a company of
people who look on riches as a seal of God's approval and
as a worthwhile goal in life.

As we search out our roots deeper in history, we find that
many major historians have seen links between the theology of the Protestant Reformation and the rise of
capitalism. The Weber thesis, proposed soon after the turn
of the century, has made a major impact on historical
thought. Weber proposed that the "spirit of capitalism"
had appeared in history as a result or by-product of the
religious ethic of Calvinism.[1] R. H. Tawney's epochal *Religion and the Rise of Capitalism* was both a refinement
and a popularization of the Weber thesis. And while a
causal link between Protestantism and capitalism is dif-

ficult to forge in a way that is utterly convincing, it has not been hard for scholars to see that the two movements, one spiritual and the other economic, have made good traveling companions. Many of the cause-effect historians who have followed in the Weber tradition have been hostile both to Protestantism and to capitalism, which certainly taints the objectivity of their work. But it is possible for us to learn from even hostile critics, and Tawney's biting comment is worth pondering:

> To countless generations of religious thinkers, the fundamental maxim of Christian social ethics had seemed to be expressed in the words of St. Paul to Timothy: "Having food and raiment, let us be therewith content. For the love of money is the root of all evil." Now [after the Reformation] . . . not sufficiency to the needs of daily life, but limitless increase and expansion, became the goal of the Christian's efforts. . . . Plunged in the cleansing waters of later Puritanism, the qualities which less enlightened ages had denounced as social vices emerged as economic virtues.[2]

The great Wesleyan revival of the eighteenth century is credited by historians as providing an all-important "brake for the untrammelled self-interest of individuals pursuing the ends of their personal and private gain."[3] Yet John Wesley himself, as an old man, warned:

> The Methodists in every place grow diligent and frugal; consequently they increase in goods. Hence they proportionably increase in pride, in anger, in the desire of the flesh, the desire of the eyes, and the pride of life. So, although the form of religion remains, the spirit is swiftly vanishing away.[4]

I hope you have "hung in" with me for this brief excursion into our history, for it is important for us to understand on what foundations our traditions and assumptions rest. It is significant for us to discover just where we are at.

To those of us who are now in young or middle adulthood, growing up as we did in the affluent post-war period in North America, the value of money has been well taught. Christianity and the accumulation of capital have seemed not only compatible, but causally linked together.

Now, however, we find ourselves living in a world for which we feel strangely unprepared. The goal of business success and the ethics of profit-making no longer seem to be completely satisfactory as an expression of a Christian life view. We live in a world in which other goals and a broader ethic are required, not only for personal spiritual survival, but for national economic survival and for global physical survival.

More and more, people at all levels of our society are talking about a closed economy. While political leaders urge restraint, a bearded, long-haired postal worker, involved against his own better judgment in a prolonged strike, says to a television interviewer: "Sure, I'd like to have more of the pie. But I guess we've all got to realize that there is only so much pie." The message is getting through. Only so much pie and the necessity of sharing it equitably: that is the greatest economic and social problem of our day. Only so much fuel, and how it should be apportioned. Only so much air, and how it can be kept breathable.

The world economy, which became apparently endlessly capable of expansion, both geographically and economically, through the discovery of half a world in the fifteenth and sixteenth centuries, and the industrial revolution of the eighteenth and nineteenth centuries, has suddenly snapped shut again. And we feel trapped in this closure. We find ourselves like the peasants in a medieval village, suddenly members of a vast "global village" in which we feel that we are, indeed, "our brothers' keepers." We know now that nonrenewable resources can be exhausted. We, as individuals and as nations, are aware that there is such a thing as debt becoming due and payable.

We sit in our living rooms and look into the "unseeing eye" of our television sets and see not just individuals but entire cities and nations going bankrupt. And at the same time we look into the empty eyes of swollen-bellied children of famine who are somehow, impossibly, still alive. And we know that somewhere, in some way, we are all personally responsible. But just sitting around with vague guilt feelings haunting us is hardly a sufficient response. We need to seriously reevaluate our whole set of life goals and to ask ourselves, "Where are we now? And where are we going?" We must put to ourselves the question worded by World Vision director, W. Stanley Mooneyham, "Is my life style supporting a famine somewhere in the world today?" We need to get back to our New Testaments and discover how truly Christian principles, enunciated by the Lord Jesus Himself and exemplified by the first-century Christians, can help us to lead the way in adapting to the new society in which we find ourselves living.

If we are, indeed, "people not content to sit back and wait in helplessness for the breakers of present and future shock to overwhelm us,"[5] we need to become actively involved in adjusting our goals, expanding our ethic, and moderating our life-style to meet the needs of this changing age. As believers in the Lord Jesus Christ, we "are all sons of light and sons of day. We are not of night nor of darkness; so then let us not sleep as others do, but let us be alert and sober" (1 Th 5:5-6, NASB).

As we study the New Testament, we understand that one of the exciting things about the attempt to bring our lives back into line with the scriptural plumbline is that Christian principles are workable in any economic structure. The New Testament does not prescribe an economic system, nor does it endorse any particular economic theories. What it does do is tell the believer how to operate within whatever economic structure, or stricture, he finds himself.

Any cinching in of our belts that we undertake will not, in the long run, hurt any of us. It is very often only when we begin to feel pinched economically that we start to sort out the debris of our things-cluttered lives and decide which things are really important and which are peripheral.

It is as citizens of a global village, a hungry global village, and perhaps as members of the last generation of the Christian Church before the return of its Lord, that we must respond. Not just intuitively, sympathetically, or guiltily. But thoughtfully and philosophically, with a firm basis in the guidelines of the Scriptures, so that we can act boldly and with conviction, not merely react to things as they happen. We must, as those who bear the name of the compassionate Jesus, exercise leadership in finding better ways to share with others. We must take our cue from the Lord Jesus Christ Himself and get a correct valuation on the things of this world.

Many years have passed since Paul wrote this warning in eager anticipation of Christ's return:

> But this I say, brethren, the time is short: it remaineth, that . . . they that buy [should be], as though they possessed not; and they that use this world, as not abusing it: for the fashion of this world passeth away (1 Co 7:29-31).

If the time was short then, it is obviously far shorter now. As Christians, we dare not sit around, rendered helpless by "future shock." Instead, we need to be quick to adapt to the new economic and social realities of our world, quick to respond lovingly to the needs of others. Only thus will we find ourselves fulfilling our Lord's command, "Occupy till I come" (Lk 19:13). Only thus can we hope to qualify for Christ's commendation, "Blessed is that servant, who his lord when he cometh shall find so doing" (Mt 24:46).

# 12

## AND WHERE WE'RE GOING!

Soon after he had returned from Cambodia, we talked with veteran missionary Norman Ens. He had been in Phnom Penh within a few days of its fall to Communism, and he not only had left all of his personal belongings but, more important, hundreds of personal friends and converts as well. He was full of the heartache of those who were left behind to face the terror of the new tyranny. Cam asked him, "Norman, when you come back home, what do you see? What strikes you about us?"

Norman was very careful in his choice of words. But he said, "I speak in churches, and people come up afterward and ask me, 'And when are you going back to Cambodia?' When I tell them, 'Oh, we're not going back to Cambodia,' they look nonplussed and ask, 'Why not?' I try to break the news gently: 'Because Cambodia is now closed to missionaries. It has fallen under communist rule.' My questioners look bewildered and drift away. 'We didn't realize—' they stammer. And I can hardly believe that people can sit—while countries, whole nations, fall—and not even know it has happened.

"To be honest with you, Cam, I see people sitting in their big chairs, watching the games on their colored TVs, unaware of what is going on around them, absorbed in the busyness of their own affairs. Sometimes I wonder if these Christians would be so engrossed in the current sports series that they would even miss the Lord's return."

Perhaps there is no more important fact by which to govern all that we do in creating our own individual lifestyles than the one that "This world is not . . . [our] home." It was by this principle that Abraham lived the life of faith, together with the other patriarchs who "confessed that they were strangers and pilgrims on the earth . . . declar-[ing] plainly that they seek a country . . . a better country, that is, an heavenly: wherefore God is not ashamed to be called their God: for he hath prepared for them a city" (Heb 11:14-16). Strangers and pilgrims. We have not time, nor have we the right, to settle down as if this world were our home. We are here only briefly.

In any age, the eyes of believers have been set beyond that horizon which is death to "a city which hath foundations, whose builder and maker is God" (Heb 11:10). For those of us who recognize the apocalyptic nature of the days in which we live, the expectation should be even clearer, more life-dominating. For our Lord pledged His word: "I go to prepare a place for you. And if I go . . . *I will come again*, and receive you unto myself; that where I am, there ye may be also" (Jn 14:2-3, itals. added). Even the short span of normal life may well be abbreviated for us by the return of Christ. How important it becomes that our lives be centered not on things, not on people, not on our own ambitions or plans, but on Jesus Christ Himself.

We know a man who is very intent on building a business empire for himself, confident that whatever he has managed to put together by the time Christ returns will be his to manage throughout eternity. But I do not read my Bible so. Jesus makes it clear that His coming will interrupt all normal activities (Mt 24:36-41) as His own are "caught

up . . . to meet the Lord in the air" (1 Th 4:17). Like the
children of Israel preparing for the Exodus, we need to
have an attitude of preparedness, "with . . . [our] loins
girded, . . . [our] shoes on . . . [our] feet, and . . . [our] staff in
. . . [our] hand" (Ex 12:11).

We live in urgent days, and our time of opportunity to
share the Gospel, to share the good things of this world,
may be very short. We need to live as people whose lives
might be suddenly cut off. We need to learn, and we *could*
learn from the Scriptures if we would come to them, the
lessons that Aleksandr Solzhenitsyn learned through his
experience of *The Gulag Archipelago*:

> What about the main thing in life, all its riddles? If you
> want, I'll spell it out for you right now. Do not pursue what
> is illusory—property and position: all that is gained at the
> expense of your nerves decade after decade, and is confis-
> cated one fell night. Live with a steady superiority over
> life—don't be afraid of misfortune and do not yearn after
> happiness. . . . Our envy of others devours us most of all.
> Rub your eyes and purify your heart—and prize above all
> else in the world those who love you and wish you well.[1]

Seven years of Soviet prison camp and many more years of
listening to the stories of hundreds of other prisoners
taught Solzhenitsyn this truth, one which even a child
could learn from the gospels, but one which we as adults
often tend to forget.

That the dark days detailed in the book of Revelation are
soon to break about this earth is all too clear. In an inter-
view filmed before his death, historian Arnold Toynbee
raised this question:

> Will man draw on the spiritual resources available from
> beyond himself—or not? On the answer to that question
> hinges the future of humanity—if there is to be one.[2]

It is no longer just the funny little man handing out Gospel

tracts who is declaring, "The end is at hand." It's just that
he knew it first.

So this is a time for uncluttered, tidied-up Christian
living. Because the Lord is "longsuffering . . . not willing
that any should perish, but that all should come to repent-
ance" (2 Pe 3:9), there may yet be some time before the
end. But events are inexorably bringing us closer to the
return of Jesus Christ. Do our hearts thrill with this anticipation? Or is there a little chill as we ponder Jesus' words,
"When the Son of man cometh, shall he find faith on the
earth?" (Lk 18:8)?

If we do, indeed, live in the last days before the return of
Jesus Christ, we are living close to the consummation of
the great purifying hope of the Church. Believers throughout the ages have lived in anticipation of the return of Jesus
Christ, and the implication of the imminence of that return
has always been:

> What sort of people ought you to be? Surely men of good
> and holy character, who live expecting and earnestly long-
> ing for the coming of the day of God (2 Pe 3:11-12, Phillips).

We can have the quiet confidence which Jesus intended
to be the distinguishing mark of His disciples in the face of
troubled times: we can obey His command to "lift up your
heads; for your redemption draweth nigh" (Lk 21:28) if,
first of all, we are sure that we are His.

I remember once thinking about the return of my Lord
and Saviour, and being troubled by the thought: "When He
comes, will I know Him? He is One whom I have loved,
sight unseen. I have only artists' conceptions on which to
base any visualization of the Lord Jesus Christ." And then
the Lord brought to my mind the verse of Scripture, "He
calleth his own sheep by name, and leadeth them out" (Jn
10:3). I realized, with a great sense of relief, that the important question was not so much "Will I know Him?" but

rather, "Will He know me?" For as long as I am known as one of His sheep, He will call me by name. What a restful confidence.

The apostle Peter invites us to "give diligence to make . . . [our]calling and election sure" (2 Pe 1:10), to take time to ascertain that we are, without doubt, participants in God's plan of redemption. And the apostle John, in his first epistle, tells us the tests by which we can validate our personal positions relative to Jesus Christ. You may wish to study that letter in detail for yourself, but I see there these three main tests by which we can examine our claims to saving faith:

1. *The test of confession of sin (1 Jn 1:5-10).* If we try to lay claim to having done the best we could, or having lived as well as the next guy, as our basis for entering God's family, we "deceive ourselves." There is only one way in which we can know the cleansing that is necessary to make us acceptable in God's sight, and that is through confession and turning from sin. If we have confessed our sins and thus experienced forgiveness and cleansing, we have passed John's first test. If not, then this is the starting point. We can feel nothing but fear at the thought of Christ's return until we have cried out, "God be merciful to me a sinner" (Lk 18:13).

2. *The test of obedience to our new Master (1 Jn 2:3-8).* Confession of sin is certainly the first step, but it is not the only one. John points out that we can know that we know Christ "if we keep his commandments" (v. 3). If we are changed persons because we live under new management, then we can face the visible, personal return of that Master, Jesus Christ, with confidence. Obedience to Christ will have two very distinct effects, as John points out:

   a. *Love (1 Jn 2:9-11).* Obedience to Christ as Lord and Master must result in an attitude of love toward our

Christian brothers and sisters as well as those in the broader brotherhood of humanity (1 Jn 3:14-19). This kind of love has inescapable economic implications!

b. *Right living (1 Jn 3:6-10).* Christ cannot be in control of a life without creating righteousness, or right living, in that individual. John is unsparing here. If we claim to have confessed our sins and thus to have entered into salvation, and then go on sinning, we're fooling only ourselves. As we abide in Christ and let His Holy Spirit give us power and direction for right living, we know "that, when he shall appear, we may have confidence, and not be ashamed before him at his coming" (1 Jn 2:28). Not that we never again sin after our initial confession, but that we do not go on and on sinning: this is the important thought here.

Again, we need to ask ourselves: "Does my life pass the test of obedience?" If not, perhaps we have never come to a point of decisively turning over our lives to the lordship of Jesus Christ. We need to reach the point where we cry out with Saul on the Damascus road, "Lord, what wilt thou have me to do?" (Ac 9:6). When we do, because He *is* Lord, He will begin to bring our lives into conformity with His life. And we can look forward to His return with joyful confidence.

3. *The test of right doctrine concerning Jesus Christ (1 Jn 4:1-4).* John makes it very clear that what we think and say of Jesus Christ is very important. After Jesus' ascension, the angelic witness was that "this same Jesus" would return (Ac 1:11). We need to reexamine the scriptural evidence concerning the nature and person of Jesus Christ; we need to assure ourselves that we are, indeed, awaiting "this same Jesus." Not some nameless force for good, not some mysterious other manifestation, not just the Kingdom of God on earth in demonstrations of love and peace

among men, but "this same Jesus." The same Jesus who was born at Bethlehem, God in human flesh; who was heard and seen and known in Galilee, the living Word; who was crucified outside of Jerusalem as the Lamb of God, the ultimate sacrifice for man's sin; who was raised from death, all His amazing claims fully vindicated in one act of enormous triumph. *This,* and no other, is the Jesus who will return in power. To be awaiting some other is to become vulnerable to the "false Christs" who, Jesus warned His disciples, would come before His own return.

Since God has ordained salvation only through His Son, Jesus Christ, right doctrine concerning Him is essential to any true experience of salvation—any experience that will pass the test.

Having set out these three crucial tests, John holds out this hope of perfect confidence to the believer: "These things have I written unto you that believe on the name of the Son of God; that ye may *know* that ye have eternal life" (1 Jn 5:13, itals. added).

We do not need to have our anticipation of Christ's return chilled by a tremor of fear if we have made sure of our relationship to Him. We can have further confidence as we look ahead if we know that our hearts are full of un-clouded love for Jesus our Lord, if we are certain that we are untrammeled by affections and desires that bind us to this temporal world.

One night, when our first baby was tiny, I lay awake thinking about the day that was past and the one that was coming, talking things over with my Lord. The day's news of world events had been particularly dismal. "Wars and rumors of wars" (Mt 24:6) could sum up the front page headlines. "Evil men . . . shall wax worse and worse" (2 Ti 3:13) would capture the mood of the other pages of the newspaper. As a new mother, I was more conscious than ever before of just what serious times we lived in. What lay ahead for my little son and for such brothers and sisters as God might bless him with?

"O Lord Jesus, how long?" I whispered. The return of the Lord was the only glimmer of light in a dark and threatening sky. And then this verse of Scripture came into my mind: "Unto them that look for him shall he appear the second time" (Heb 9:28).

My heart was troubled as I pondered those words. "Lord," I asked, "am I really looking for Your appearing? Most of the day I am washing or ironing, cooking meals or changing diapers. O Lord, I wouldn't want to miss You!" I must have drifted off to sleep then.

Suddenly I found myself in the village bank, a familiar place where I went each month to deposit Cam's check and transact our personal business. The faces were all familiar: Doreen and Sheila and Marg all calling a friendly "Hello" as I entered the busy but informal atmosphere of the building. I parked the stroller against a wall where Geoff, our little firstborn, could enjoy the sights and sounds of this fascinating new world, and then I went to the counter. There, with the assistant manager, I began to review our investments. Our safety deposit box was brought out, and I considered the timing of converting some stocks and bonds to more recent issues. Then, as I was considering what would be the most profitable thing to do, something happened.

There was no visible change, no audible sound, and yet suddenly I knew that everything was different. Nothing was holding me down. I was free to go! I could meet the Lord in the air! I didn't float upward; I just knew that I could go to be with my Saviour.

As that consciousness dawned on me with all of the clarity of a trumpet call, I pushed my bonds across the counter to the banker. "Here, Bob," I said excitedly, "you can have them. I won't need them anymore." And then, as I felt my newly constituted body begin to move toward the magnet pull of the returning Lord Jesus, I reached down and lifted my little son from his stroller. "Lord," I breathed, "You promised me Geoff. I can't go without him!" With Geoff in my arms, I rushed out of the building into the street. Together then, my little son and I rose to meet our Lord. We would meet Cam there, I knew, and all earthly things were left gladly and unhesitatingly behind.

I awakened from my dream to hear my husband breathing regularly, deep in sleep. I listened for the baby. Yes, we were all still here on earth. But I knew from the response of my heart that no earthly thing held me. And I knew with a certainty that has never left me since, that I would hear or feel the call, the change, the quickening, or the release, whatever it would be that would signal my freedom to leave the duties of this earth and go to meet my Lord and Saviour Jesus Christ.

I was flooded with peace as I whispered, "Even so, come, Lord Jesus" (Rev 22:20).

It is in the confidence of Christ's return that we face a threatening future. It is in the confidence that we are His that we embrace and declare this glad hope. And it is in the light of this that we affirm our position as "strangers and pilgrims on the earth" (Heb 11:13). Occupied with the day-to-day tasks of earning a living and making a home, concerned with the responsible conserving and sharing of this world's goods, we nonetheless live in the glad expectancy of His return. Maranatha!

# NOTES

## First, This Word

1. James Boswell, *Boswell's Life of Johnson*, vol. 1. (Oxford: Clarendon, 1934).

## Chapter 1

1. Francis Schaeffer, *Pollution and the Death of Man: The Christian View of Ecology* (Wheaton, Ill.: Tyndale, 1972), p. 85.
2. Charles A. Reich, *The Greening of America* (New York: Random House, Bantam Books, 1971).

## Chapter 2

1. Stanley Tam with Ken Anderson, *God Owns My Business* (Waco, Tex.: Word, 1969), p. 112.
2. Harold J. Sutton, "Immortal Money: A Study of Tithing," *Alliance Witness*, Mar. 17, 1965, p. 5.

## Chapter 3

1. David Grayson, *Adventures in Contentment* (New York: Grosset & Dunlap, 1906), p. 3.
2. Ibid., p. 12.

## Chapter 5

1. "How Not to Have a Garage Sale," *Christianity Today*, July 1974.
2. Robert Schuller, *Move Ahead with Possibility Thinking* (Old Tappan, N.J.: Revell, Spire Books, 1973), p. 107.
3. "A Way to Keep Your Debts Under Control," *Reader's Digest*, May 1969. Condensed from *Changing Times*, Feb. 1969, p. 37.

## Chapter 6

1. C. S. Lewis, *Mere Christianity* (London: Fontana Books, 1970), pp. 77-78.
2. Ronald J. Sider, "A Modest Proposal for Christian Giving in a Starving World: The Graduated Tithe," *Theology, News and Notes*, Oct. 1975, p. 15.
3. John Wesley, *Works*, as quoted by Kemper Fullerton, "Calvinism and Capitalism," in *Protestantism and Capitalism: The Weber Thesis and Its Critics*, ed. Robert W. Green (Boston: D. C. Heath, 1959).

## Chapter 7

1. Edith Redman, *Recipes for Healthier Children: A Mother's Guide* (Tannersville, Pa.: Tandem, 1973); and *Recipes for a Healthier Family* (Toronto: Gage, 1975).
2. Stephen Board, "Six Billion People Are Coming to Dinner," *His*, June 1975, p. 12.
3. This figure is from the pamphlet, *UNICEF Is . . .*, published by UNICEF.
4. Christie Harris and Moira Johnston, *Fig Leafing Through History* (New York: Atheneum, 1971).

## CHAPTER 8

1. Robinson Jeffers, "Shine, Perishing Republic," *American Literature Survey, The Twentieth Century* (New York: Viking, 1962).

## CHAPTER 9

1. A. W. Tozer, *I Talk Back to the Devil* (Harrisburg, Pa.: Christian Pubns., 1972), p. 29.
2. Tozer, *The Root of the Righteous* (Harrisburg, Pa.: Christian Pubns., 1955), p. 25.
3. Charles H. Spurgeon, *Faith's Checkbook* (Chicago: Moody, n.d.), p. 160.
4. Harold Lindsell, "Advice to Young Evangelicals," *Moody Monthly*, Oct. 1975.
5. John Brooks, review of John Kenneth Galbraith, *Money, Whence It Came, Where It Went* in *Book-of-the-Month Club News*, Oct. 1975.

## CHAPTER 10

1. Shakespeare *Hamlet* 1.5.263.
2. Walter Stewart, "Canada's Credo: Honesty Pays," *Reader's Digest*, June 1971, p. 27.
3. Ibid., p. 30.
4. C. S. Lewis, *The Screwtape Letters* (London: Fontana Books, 1970), p. 109.
5. A. W. Tozer, *The Pursuit of God* (Harrisburg, Pa.: Christian Pubns., 1948), pp. 21 ff.
6. A. B. Simpson, "Himself," in *Hymns of the Christian Life* (Harrisburg, Pa.: Christian Pubns., 1936), no. 154.
7. F. Green, "My Goal Is God," in *Hymns of the Christian Life* (Harrisburg, Pa.: Christian Pubns., 1936), no. 351.

## CHAPTER 11

1. Robert W. Green, *Protestantism and Capitalism: The Weber Thesis and Its Critics* (Boston: D. C. Heath, 1959), p. vii.
2. R. H. Tawney, *Religion and the Rise of Capitalism* (New York: Mentor Books, New Amer. Library, 1954), p. 206.
3. Marquis W. Childs and Douglass Cater, *Ethics in a Business Society* (New York: Mentor Books, New Amer. Library, 1954), p. 55.
4. From John Wesley, *Works*, as quoted by J. H. Plumb, *England in the Eighteenth Century*, vol. 7, The Pelican History of England (London: Penguin Books, 1963), p. 97. Plumb's chapter, "John Wesley and the Road to Salvation," pp. 91-97, is most interesting. Wesley did not, however, consider the situation as hopeless as his quotation might suggest. The remedy he suggested, that "those who gain all they can and save all they can . . . also give all they can" has already been quoted in chap. 7.

The author also suggests reading these books: W. S. Mooneyham, *What Do You Say to a Hungry World?* (Waco, Tex.: Word, 1975; and Sherwood Wirt, *The Social Conscience of the Evangelical* (New York: Harper & Row, 1968).

## CHAPTER 12

1. Aleksandr I. Solzhenitsyn, *The Gulag Archipelago* (New York: Harper & Row, 1974), p. 591.
2. "The Prospects for Humanity," with Arnold J. Toynbee, Canadian Broadcasting Corp., Oct. 27, 1975.